ENOUGH IS ENOUGH

The Explosion in Los Angeles
America Receives a Wake-Up Call

MYCHAL WYNN

ENOUGH IS ENOUGH

The Explosion in Los Angeles
America Receives a Wake-Up Call

RISING SUN PUBLISHING
P.O. Box 70906
Marietta, Georgia 30007
(800) 524-2813

Mychal Wynn is also the author of
Empowering African-American Males to Succeed
Don't Quit – Inspirational Poetry

FIRST EDITION, 1993
ISBN 1–880463–33–4, cloth
ISBN 1–880463–34–2, paper

Enough is Enough.

Rising Sun Publishing
P.O. Box 70906
Marietta, Georgia 30007
(404) 518-0369
(800) 524-2813

Printed in the United States of America.

This book is written in an effort to bring about a better understanding of the differing realities that contributed to the anger, frustration, and rage that exploded on April 29, 1992 and what we must do to prevent urban America from exploding again.

CONTENTS

Introduction

My wife, our three year old son and I moved out of our four bedroom home in the Los Angeles California suburban community of Carson less than two months before the twelve men and women were to return verdicts that would erupt a volcano which had been dormant since the 1965 Watts riots.

The Carson community, which includes many upper middle class black families, borders the economically impoverished communities of Compton and Watts, two of the many bordering Los Angeles communities besieged by violence following the not guilty verdicts in the trail of four white Los Angeles police officers charged with the use of excessive force in the videotaped beating of Rodney King, a black man stopped for speeding.

Sociologists, psychologists, community leaders, political leaders, and people from every walk of life have talked about the verdicts, and the violence which followed, that claimed over 60 lives in the Los Angeles area. A special commission has issued a report critical of former police chief Daryl Gates and the administration of Los Angeles Mayor Tom Bradley in their failure to prepare for, and respond to, the violence. Thousands of people were injured or arrested and over a billion dollars in property damaged was done to homes and businesses which were looted and burned. They have attributed the explosion to single parent homes, poverty, failed government programs, organized gang activities, or as one of the jurors said, "These people just needed an excuse to loot."

While many political and civic leaders appeared impotent in responding to the rage Oprah Winfrey, Montell Williams, Arsenio Hall and others hosted talk shows through which people tried to understand the verdicts and explain the anger and violence that followed. Evidence in the dialogue on all of the talk shows was that the pain and frustration of urban America had reached the critical boiling point. With the notable exceptions of Congresswoman Maxine Waters and State Senator Diane Watson, federal, state, and local politicians lacked the necessary understanding and leadership to calm the explosion. Talk show host Arsenio Hall offered a sharp contrast to America's stereotype. A young black man provided the understanding and leadership that most in our government lacked. He went into the community to attempt to calm the storm and awaken those lost and forgotten souls from their nightmare.

This book shares the perspective of a black man in America who understands the pain, frustration, feelings of powerlessness, hopelessness, and despair experienced daily by those forgotten in urban America. I lived with the daily stress, tension, frustration, and pain growing up in the segregated black ghetto of Chicago's South Side. In a community of few jobs and little hope, of vacant lots and public housing. A place like South-Central Los Angeles, where gun shots and police sirens play taps each night over the souls of our children. Where those who survive live with the terror and nightmares of friends and family lying in pools of blood. A place where there are only victims. Police who are placed into a combat zone. Teachers who receive battle pay. Parents who pray each day that their children survive their journey to and from school. And children, whose dreams fade each day under the pain and hopelessness of their communities.

Unlike most of my friends, relatives, and classmates I escaped the death and despair of urban America. Where my daily prayer during my last year at Chicago's DuSable high school (a year in which Chicago had the highest murder rate in the country) was, "Please God, let me live long enough to leave here." My prayer would be answered as I would survive America's urban jungle to go on and graduate with honors from the predominately white Northeastern University during Boston's racially tense and often violent early days of court ordered school busing.

Educated, professionally and financially successful I have had a corporate career spanning some of America's largest companies; Arthur Andersen & Company; IBM; and Transamerica. As a successful upper middle class black entrepreneur, an author and publisher, I am a member of W.E.B. DuBois' talented tenth. Dr. DuBois prophesied that at least ten percent of black America would achieve an education enabling them to succeed in America. He envisioned that with that education we would move throughout the larger society eventually utilizing our tools, talents, and resources to uplift and provide hope for the entire black community. The black middle class has in fact exceeded Dr. DuBois' prophecy in terms of educational and economic gains. We have not however, achieved Dr. DuBois' vision of applying our tools, talents, and resources to build a bridge between the black middle and upper class and the nation's black underclass.

I find myself on the bridge between a generation of older blacks who fought for civil rights and a generation of younger blacks who proudly wear the symbols of Malcolm X and preach a new revolution from the racism, oppression, and victimization of America's underclass. It is their frustration, their feelings of powerlessness, and their rage that has exploded and is inextricably tied to their slogan, "No justice, no peace."

In my book, *"Empowering African-America Males to Succeed: A Ten-Step Approach for Parents and Teachers,"* I outlined strategies for parents and teachers to help African-American young men develop the character, consciousness, and vision to succeed. To prepare them for the inevitable injustice, racism and oppression that they would encounter in this society. And, to empower their spirits and their consciousness, to take advantage of the undeniable opportunities that others have found in America. However, the workshops that I present to teachers in school districts throughout the country reveals the personal frustration, lack of understanding, and inability to identify with the sense of hopelessness, frustration, and rage that has consumed so many of our young people.

Many of the teachers are representative of the Simi Valley juror who suggested that Rodney King, a black man, was responsible for his own brutal beating at the hands of the white officers. An attitude pervasive in America where we blame the victim for his or her victimization. Our criminal justice system overflows with black, Latino, and other minorities. The reality of this juror is that minorities in general, and blacks in particular, are inherently prone to violence. A reality shared by many whites who felt that the beating was not racially motivated. A reality that convinces them that whites don't treat blacks like that anymore. Many in white America deny the racism, sexism, hatred, and bigotry, which like a cancer continues to eat away at America in general, and the minority community in particular.

Many black leaders, journalist, government officials, and psychological experts were interviewed following the first day of violence. Oprah Winfrey broadcasted a show from Los Angeles representing a multi-ethnic multi-economic cross-section of people from the community; community activists; parents; young men and women; black and Korean store owners and others. An hour after all of the shouting, finger pointing, and praying was done no perspectives had changed. They, the Simi Valley jurors, the many teachers I've worked with, and like so many in America watching the news broadcasts from the streets of Los Angeles, saw a different reality and few sought understanding.

Many of those interviewed have talked about the healing process, but what about the process of riding our justice system of its racist and oppressive treatment of minorities and poor people? Many have talked about the savage actions of those involved in the violent aftermath of the verdicts, but what about riding our society of the savage actions of policemen, hate groups, and individuals who perpetuate savage violence on minorities and women each day in America? Many have talked about the people in impoverished areas throughout urban America taking care of themselves and making their communities better, but what about those of us who have the education, financial resources, and management skills working to make all of America greater? Not just suburban America, or white America, or middle class black America.

This book shares my perspective, my vision, and my reality.

Chapter 1

Differing realities

In November, 1991, I left my Carson, California home for the daily commute to my job as a computer systems consultant at the Transamerica Occidental Life Insurance Company, located on the fringes of the Los Angeles downtown business district. I often drove along Broadway boulevard, a journey through South-Central to downtown Los Angeles which offered an escape from the stop and go traffic on the 110 freeway.

I stopped my black Mercedes-Benz 300E at a traffic light at Century Boulevard and Broadway. A white Los Angeles motorcycle policeman stopped alongside me. A black man, driving a black Mercedes-Benz, with black tinted windows, in South-Central Los Angeles lives in a different reality from the many whites in expensive cars who also make the daily commute along Broadway.

As we pulled away from the traffic light, the officer pulled away at barely 15 miles per hour. I knew that he was allowing me to get in front of him so that he could run my license plate, searching for an expired registration or an outstanding warrant.

Surely a black man driving a Benz in South-Central

Los Angeles was doing something illegal. As he continued his snail's pace the distance between us increased as I reached the posted speed limit of 35 miles per hour.

The inevitable occurred as I approached the next major intersection, Manchester boulevard. In my rear view mirror I could see the flashing lights of his motorcycle as he quickly closed the roughly three block distance between us. After I pulled over, in my rearview mirror I could see the officer walking toward my car with his hand on his gun. I prepared myself for what, as a black man in America, would become a life-threatening encounter.

I consciously placed both of my hands on the top of the steering wheel. I sat still as the officer approached my driver's side window. With his hand still on his gun, he yelled at me, "Do you know how fast you were going?" I told him that I was driving 35 miles per hour, to which he angrily responded, "Give me your driver's license."

I told him that it was in my coat pocket hanging behind my seat in the rear of the car and I *"asked him"* if I could get it!

My reality told me to make it clear to this officer that I wasn't going to give him any excuse to end my life. I knew that encounters between black men and policemen in America far too often end in tragedy for black men. White America is comforted by the newspaper reports of white officers who tell their stories of how black men, with careers and families, without reason or provocation become so violent that police must beat and shoot them. Stories of how black men, without criminal records, or any logical reasons to resist, are accused of engaging in violent struggles for the policemen's guns resulting in their own executions.

I knew that despite my having a three-year-old son, a wife, a business, a career and everything to live for, that this officer, and others like him throughout America, needed little provocation to blow my brains out. After which, he could simply report strange and violent behavior on my part and his report could go virtually uncontested in a society which wants to believe that policemen, particularly white policemen, are honorable men of high moral standards and that black men are dangerous and prone to violence. Even if it would reach a Grand Jury investigation, the reality of white America, like the Simi Valley juror, would have convinced them that because I was a black man I had brought it on myself. That, like Rodney King, I would have in some way been responsible for my own beating and, or, execution.

The whites driving their expensive cars, at speeds exceeding 60 miles per hour, during their daily commute along this South-Central boulevard lived in a different reality. They would have questioned the officer's attitude and rudeness. They may have responded in a harsh tone of voice themselves and openly expressed their annoyance. The reality of upper middle class white executives would cause them to see this encounter as simply threatening their automobile insurance premiums.

The reality of the aristocracy, who believe policemen to be the public servants they are, may have caused them to respond emotionally to the arrogance and rudeness of this officer as did Zsa Zsa Gabor who reportedly slapped a Beverly Hills police officer as a result of his belligerent behavior after stopping her for an expired registration on her Rolls Royce.

Extreme, maybe, but their reality would not have caused them to perceive a routine traffic stop as a life-threatening encounter. They would not have had to reflect back upon the lessons in life like those that my father had taught me. About how to speak to policemen, "Yes sir, no sir." About how to avoid becoming openly angry, even if they used the "N" word. No, the whites driving their cars along Broadway boulevard would not have had flashbacks of the horrible brutality and victimization of blacks and other minorities which occurs daily in this society by men with guns and badges.

For members of the minority community in America, an encounter with law enforcement is one that we like to avoid. Not because we all have something to hide, but because we all have something to lose, our lives.

Although a well educated, articulate, and financially affluent black man, my reality had been shaped by America's racism and oppression long before the Rodney King videotape. It taught me that this officer's reality could have been shaped by any number of experiences, perceptions, and prejudices.

Prejudices that stereotype black men driving expensive cars as drug dealers and pimps or engaged in other criminal activities.

That black people in general are not entitled to the same rights and freedoms as those of he, his family, and friends.

That years of experience with inarticulate, uneducated, and poor minorities has shaped his perception that we are all that way.

Perhaps in me he saw the people he, his family, friends, and fellow officers had come to dislike and despise. Perhaps he lived in a community like Simi Valley, 99% white. Where blacks are allowed to venture into daily to cut the grass and clean the houses as long as they leave before sunset. Like communities throughout America whose residents watch the nightly newscasts of the crime and violence that plagues urban America contributing to their reality that, "those people" must be brutally controlled.

Perhaps as he approached my car he prepared himself for the worst based upon a distorted perception of black men. A perception shaped as a child where his parents and their friends used the "N" word as they sought to degrade and dehumanize people who were simply ethnically and culturally different from themselves. Maybe he had attended one of the many predominately white schools where coaches pump up their teams with racist locker room pep talks about the ensuing game with black teams. An attitude that had been encouraged and further defined in his police locker room where racist jokes about blacks and other minorities were openly expressed. Encouraged by those who laughed and condoned by those who remained silent. In his mind I was not a human being, not citizen that he was sworn to serve, but simply a black man in a Benz.

Maybe that's why he approached my car with his hand on his gun. Maybe that's why the rude and belligerent way in which he spoke to me seem to play the same song that blacks and other minorities in America hear over and over. That we are in some way less important, less worthy, and less likely to be treated with the dignity and respect afforded America's white citizens.

After giving him my driver's license, being careful to restrict my movements, to avoid intimidating eye contact, to avoid expressing my annoyance and simmering anger, he returned to his motorcycle. Some 15 minutes later he returned with my ticket. This was the first time that he even told me why I had been stopped.

For driving 55 miles per hour!

As he walked away I felt the same sense of relief felt by many in urban America. The encounter was over and I had not become another brutal victim. But as I sat there in my car I also felt the anger. An anger that tears away your flesh from the inside. That slaps you in the face and says, "Wake up boy!" Not only must you deal with all of the same stress that others deal with; crime; paying your bills; providing for your children's education; working; family problems and the like, you must deal with the real dangers of violence under the color of authority.

Unlike many who allow their anger to fester inside of them, to kindle a fire that explodes into an uncontrollable rage that causes a violent reaction. A reaction that too frequently catches our families and friends in the crossfire. My anger became focused as I continued my drive to work. I was determined that I would come face to face with that officer again. Not on a street corner but in court. Yes, no matter what the outcome, I would have my day and I would have my say!

When the officer appeared in court he fabricated a story of how I sped past him while he was driving 35 miles per hour. He told the judge of how he allows drivers leeway of upwards of 10 miles above the posted speed limit and that I had driven by him so fast that he had to stop me. From his expressions and tone of voice as he told his lie it was evident that he lived in a reality shared by many policemen. A reality in which officers know that many black, Hispanic, and other minorities are intimidated by our court system and cannot articulate and defend themselves before officers who have learned to speak clearly, articulately, and with conviction to judges and juries. A reality in which we know that most often it is simply our word against theirs.

In the minds and reality of many judges and juries those who represent the law are assumed honorable and of high integrity. Whereas black, Hispanic, and other minorities represent the lawlessness in America and are assumed liars. If you do not speak english, speak in broken english, or experience any difficulty telling your story you have even less creditability in our courts. Policemen know that our complaints of the unfair, improper, and often brutal treatment directed at us are seldom taken seriously by the district attorney's office, rarely investigated by their fellow policemen, and hardly ever result in punishment by our courts. The only stories that receive any attention at all are those resulting in death, or captured on videotape!

What was the reality of the officers who were video-taped savagely beating Rodney King?

The same officers who were overheard boasting, bragging, and laughing about the whipping that they had given this black man, "That was one of the worse beatings that I have given anyone in a while." Officers who spoke of a black domestic dispute which they had responded to earlier as, "Right out of Gorillas in the mist." Officers who were said to have repeatedly used racial slurs while they stomped and beat him with their batons.

Did their reality reflect that the brutalization and victimization of the underclass (to which blacks, no matter how well educated and affluent, are inextricably tied) enjoys a level of social acceptance in their Simi Valley-like communities throughout America? Perhaps their reality was that they have become the overseers and that America's inner cities are the plantation fields where violent and brutal lessons must be taught those who dare challenge their authority. One of the officers referred to Rodney King as a Mandingo, a popular racist reference to big black men (the Mandingo people were among the early African tribes captured and brought to America during the slave trade).

Unlike the whites driving through South-Central, this is my reality.

When I spoke to the judge I easily and articulately destroyed the officer's story. I described all of the details of that morning. Of how the officer had stopped alongside me. How it was impossible to drive at 55 miles per hour in that particular stretch of Broadway boulevard because of the synchronized traffic signals during rush hour traffic. I described how he had approached my car and for a brief moment I had a forum to tell our story. A story of how black people in general, and black men in particular, are treated by police officers and sheriff deputies in America. Although this was only traffic court it helped to eased my pain as I looked at the expression on the officer's face as I told my story. My case was dismissed, but what of the next black man in a Benz?

*　　*　　*

We live in a society where, if the victim is engaged in an alleged criminal activity, or has a previous criminal record, they dare not complain about police harassment and brutality. To do so places them in real fear of continuing harassment and being placed on trial themselves should their complaint go to court. Perhaps if they remain determined and insist on filing a formal complaint, and successfully run the gauntlet of police and investigators who attempt to intimidate them from pursuing their complaint, they may have the good fortune of having their complaint taken seriously. However, they must have the courage to undergo a personal investigation, and the resources to endure the inconvenience and financial hardship that result from our judicial process.

They must face the resulting court proceedings in which they discover that the issue of their victimization must withstand the reality test of judges and juries. Where more and more people in this country have accepted a reality that sanctions the uncivilized, barbaric, racist, bigoted, and criminal behavior of policemen, under the color of authority. Their reality rationalizes such behavior as resulting from the tough job that policemen have to do, and The failure of the criminal justice system at keeping criminals off of the streets. A reality that concludes that black, Hispanic, and other minorities are more prone to commit crimes and bring this type of brutality upon themselves.

The videotaped beating of Rodney King traumatized the world. The not guilty verdicts of the policemen who brutally beat him numbed America. Yet one of the jurors after watching the same videotape that shocked the world stated that

Rodney King, the victim, brought it, the victimization and beating, upon himself. That in her mind, "He clearly controlled the situation." Despite the videotaped account of the three policemen who surrounded him like a pack of wild animals, viciously swinging their batons 59 times, breaking bones, and piercing flesh. It's her reality, and that of millions of others like her, that has created this twisted system of justice in America.

*   *   *

South-Central Los Angeles, like many inner-city communities throughout the country, has been alienated and separated. Living a reality misunderstood by white America and disconnected from middle class black America.

The reality of an area of South-Central Los Angeles, called the Jungle, is that of drive-by shootings, drugs, poverty, welfare and despair. Yet, up the hill, only a few blocks away in the exclusive upper middle class black community of Baldwin Hills, is a reality of million dollar homes. Owned by successful, educated, professional blacks preoccupied with property values, financial portfolios, cocktail parties, and political fundraisers. Where parents shun their children's association with poor blacks. So much so that there was once talk of constructing a fence totally surrounding the community to protect and to isolate themselves from the blacks stuck at the bottom of the hill.

Many of its elite and middle class black residents are afraid of the blacks who live in South-Central Los Angeles, Compton, and Watts. Like Los Angeles' white community, for many of them, their contact with the impoverished underclass only occurs when logistics requires them to drive their expensive cars through those communities.

I've been at social gatherings of middle class blacks

where there's an intellectual analysis of the problems plaguing America's black underclass. Their reality becomes a reflection of white America where the problems are blamed on the victims. They argue that blacks at the very bottom of the educational, social, and economic ladder need simply to accept responsibility for themselves. They should simply get off of their lazy butts and get a job. They should open their own stores, clean up their own communities, and stop selling and using drugs. They don't have to live on welfare. No one is forcing them to behave in the way in which they're behaving.

Like their white counterparts, their reality concludes that the patient must become the doctor. Responsible for diagnosing and operating on his or her own ailment without the education, sophistication, equipment, medicines, research assistance, or support mechanisms to do so. And even if the patient successfully operates on his or her own tumor, before they can gain the strength to stand on their own they are beaten down again. The road that they must travel is lined with drug dealers who offer a release from their pain and frustration. Politicians who parade through their communities like used car salesmen promising much but delivering little. The check cashing outlets who eagerly cash their welfare and social security checks with extortion-like fees. And the store owners who offer inferior products and high prices for those trapped in urban America.

As families begin to stand together they are driven apart by a welfare system that abandons them if the father stays at home and helps the family to gather its meager resources to uplift themselves. Urban America has been abandoned by failed politicians who discard job programs while continuing welfare programs. Politicians who fail to implement anything while they argue and debate the effectiveness of enterprise zones and community empowerment programs.

America, in large part thanks to the media, has

accepted a stereotype that blacks and Hispanics are lazy and simply don't want to do better for themselves. That they choose to exist on welfare and live in decaying, crime-ridden communities and that their cries of institutional racism and police brutality are unfounded excuses for their condition.

It's time to wake up America!

There are black, Hispanic, and other minorities all over America working to uplift themselves from America's urban jungles. Yet with each step forward they are pushed, dragged, or beaten two steps backward. Children who push themselves through school enduring the constant stress and dangers of our inner cities. Attempting to escape the threats of urban America's violence which claims more of their young lives each day. Mothers struggling as heads of households on meager paychecks doing the best that they can to keep their sons out of gangs and their daughters from joining the next generation of babies having babies. And men working to free themselves and their families from America's urban nightmare, yet, who carry all of America's worse labels. Irresponsible, gang banger, pimp, dope dealer, dope user, lazy, stupid, need I go on? No matter how hard they try there will always be a social worker, store owner, salesperson, or policeman to remind them of their uselessness to America.

When blacks and Hispanics are out of work, white America believes it's because we're lazy. When white America is out of work their reasons are many. Unfair foreign competition; a declining economy; declining demand; or affirmative action!

When blacks and Hispanics, historically denied equal access to educational, vocational, and professional opportunities, collect welfare and unemployment they are a burden on honest tax payers. When whites collect welfare and unemployment they demand that the Federal Government increase the taxpayer burden by; extending unemployment benefits; subsidizing the farming of products that we don't need and artificially increasing the prices of the products that we do need; continue to spend billions of dollars on military weapons, insuring our ability to destroy the world, so that we maintain their unneeded military related jobs; and loosening environmental protection in industries that threaten to make the planet a wasteland to further protect their jobs.

The reality is that those who are the first to criticize programs designed to help those who exist in America's urban ghettos are the most active in lobbying their own form of welfare. For many in white America, despite their accessibility to every opportunity within this society they refuse to put forth the effort to gain new knowledge and expand their skills enabling them to acquire jobs and develop businesses in industries that will help to build a stronger America.

It's the selfishness of America that has shaped the reality of those stuck at the bottom of the hill. A reality that tells them that those outside of their community don't care and that those within their community are unable to develop the collective consciousness to do better for themselves. That those who attempt to stand up, work hard, and try to free themselves from America's urban nightmare are beaten back by drug dealers and gang bangers while the best policemen and resources are directed at the problems occurring uptown. Cornered into their despair by insurance and bank red-lining. Each day they seem to fight their battle alone. They feel themselves hopelessly trapped. Powerless to free themselves from the seemingly endless cycle of poverty and despair. White America has discarded them, and black America has abandoned them.

*   *   *

Each year black America's clergy, fraternities, sororities, doctors, dentists, lawyers, bankers, accountants, engineers, newspaper publishers, educators, and numerous community organizations, journey to Los Angeles or urban communities like Los Angeles for their annual meetings. The urban eye sores are removed from the convention sites where conventioneers spend millions of dollars each year. Not only does precious little of the money that they spend go toward breaking the impoverish cycles of urban communities, in some cases just a few blocks away, but there is little contact between black America's professional elite and black America's underclass.

In South-Central Los Angeles there are no National Medical Association health clinics, no National Bar Association legal assistance centers, no National Urban Bankers loan packaging offices, no National Association of Black Accountants programs on managing your money and breaking the cycle of poverty, and no National Association of Black MBAs small business management and marketing programs.

Although many of these, together with other black organizations, fund some type of scholarship programs and maintain various types of local community outreach programs, blacks in areas like South-Central Los Angeles have precious little contact with America's black elite.

This is not a condemnation of America's black middle class, only a view of the differing realities that has left America's black underclass feeling angry, frustrated, and powerless. With the condemnation of white America, and the alienation from middle class black America, the urban underclass stands alone.

The media has desensitize us to its violence and despair. We have stopped asking ourselves what we, as a collective America, can do to end the cycle of hopelessness. To stop the drugs, gangs, and violence that continues to destroy our inner cities. We have instead turned our attention and resources to what we can do to control the inner cities. To limit the violence to the inner cities, thus protecting our suburban and hilltop enclaves.

We have followed the example of our prison system. Not one of rehabilitation but one of removal. Not one of replacing the hopelessness and despair with visions of direction and opportunity but one of treating the sickness by removing the sore.

America's debate over the capital gains tax perpetuates the ridiculous Reagan-Bush trickle-down theory. Help the wealthy become wealthier and something is bound to trickle down to the poor? Like the Simi Valley juror, Reagan, Bush, and much of the leadership in America live in a different reality.

The wealthy already have a wealth consciousness, the poor desperately need one. The wealthy know how to take what they have and build on it. How to research information and put their ideas into action. How to leverage their resources to take advantage of the available opportunities and how to create opportunities where none exist. Instead of allocating time, energy, and resources to help the wealthy make more money through a reduction in the Capital Gains tax we should provide incentives for the wealthy (who bring with them their wealth consciousness) to invest in the rebuilding and retraining of urban America. Those existing in urban America are in desperate need of providing for their families today, they cannot rest on the hope that something, someday, will trickle down! By encouraging the wealthy through tax incentives, low interest loans, and other incentives to invest in urban America we would provide much needed jobs and better communities today.

We must help the poor to develop a wealth consciousness. Helping them to build businesses and homes in their communities will develop a sense of ownership in the community. We must build the foundation of the community. Who ever heard of building a house from the top down?

America's underclass is unconcerned with whether interest rates go up or down, but of how to stretch their welfare checks, which America openly despises them for receiving, to provide for the basic needs of their families. They're not concerned with the events in South America, the Soviet Union, or the Persian Gulf, but of how they can give their children hope when surrounded by so much despair.

They are angry that the American government can spend billions of dollars cleaning up the mess created by affluent white men who have destroyed our savings and loans while there is no money to build parks, recreation centers, affordable housing, or job training programs to offer them hope of a brighter tomorrow while easing the pain of today. They are angry that everyone from the government assistance offices, to the non-black-owned businesses, to law enforcement treats them with disrespect and disregard. They have become the forgotten and the despised.

Each blow struck against Rodney King represented more than the racist, savage attack of white police officers. Each blow was symbolic of America's disregard of their problems. Like Rodney King, they lay helpless in our urban communities. Powerless to fend off the blows. As Rodney King barely survived, so too do they, disconnected from America. This is their reality.

*   *   *

Violence perpetuated in urban communities throughout America has overburdened our courts, our jails, our patience and has become the movie scripts for America's evening entertainment.

The jurors watched the videotaped beating of Rodney King over and over, frame by frame, at regular speed, and in slow motion, until they became numb to the violence. Their view of reality required them to search within each frame past the obvious, to something that would explain why these white policemen would behave in a way which the world found barbaric and uncivilized. These were the type of people whom they socialize with, see at the local grocery store, coach their son's soccer team, and who attend their churches.

Surely there was something in this black man's behavior, one of America's underclass, from the communities that they have tried to escape, that demanded such force. This criminal had taken their civil guardians, their fellow church-goers, on a dangerous and perilous high speed chase. He must have done something which demanded that their respectable neighbors viciously swing their batons and surround him like wild, savage animals, striking blow after blow. Eventually, their reality required that they reach the conclusion that Rodney King was not the victim and that the four police officers were simply performing the duty that we in America had charged them with. Their reality suggested that what the world saw was an aberration, as stated by then Los Angeles Police Chief Daryl Gates following the initial news broadcasts of the graphically brutal videotaped beating.

Their reality convinced them that this black man possessed super human strength that would have allowed him to rise up and threaten the lives of the 15 to 20 police officers witnessing the beating. Their reality was not unlike those who called into radio and television talk shows following the initial broadcast of the videotape. They expressed their sense of frustration over the courts' inability to protect them from the crime and violence in America. A violence which is most often associated with the character and behavior of minorities.

A reality that caused them to question, "If Rodney King wasn't guilty of something, why did he try to elude the police?"

"When he got out of the car, why didn't he simply lay down as the police said they told him too?"

"After all, he was the criminal, the police were only doing their job."

Their reality also required that they defend the officers, by arguing that the chase left the officers with their adrenaline pumped. They were tense and out of control. Yet, if Rodney King wouldn't have tried to get away, the officers wouldn't have been so pumped up, therefore it was still his fault.

In the reality of blacks and other minorities the videotape of these four officers viciously beating this black man represented an all to common occurrence of violence directed, under the color of authority, toward minorities in America. In our reality, these four white policemen were not of our neighbors, they weren't part of our social circle, they didn't represent the guardians of our society but the legal oppressors. Charged with protecting suburban white America from urban black America, by any means necessary.

In the minority community we understood that each blow struck against Rodney King could have been struck against any of us no matter what the circumstances. We know that it doesn't need to be a high speed chase but simply a routine traffic stop, a domestic dispute, being in the wrong neighborhood, or a case of mistaken identity.

The reality in black America reflects the evidence of a society which has demonstrated in the courts, in the media, through governmental action and inaction, that the lives of blacks and other minorities are in some way less valuable.

Our reality tells us that if the brutal and vicious attack of three black police officers against a white man was

graphically captured on videotape that justice would be swift
and the penalties severe. That, in our wildest imaginations we
cannot conceive of an all black jury anywhere in America
being allowed to sit in judgment over blacks charged with
committing violence against whites!

*   *   *

The reality of those in the minority community of Los
Angeles had been shaped through such events as:

Eulia Love, a 39 year old black woman, killed by Los
Angeles Police who claimed that she threatened them with a
butcher knife. Shot 12 times following a dispute over a
delinquent gas bill.

Pouvi Tualaulelei and Itali Tualaulelei, two Samoan
brothers, killed by a Compton Police officer following a
domestic dispute. Pouvi was shot 12 times, 8 of which were in
the back and his brother, Itali, was shot eight times, 5 of which
were in the back. Each, shot while kneeling on the ground.

Arturo Jiminez, a 19 year old Hispanic youth, killed by
Los Angeles County Sheriff deputies. Unarmed, yet shot three
times in the chest.

Steven Clemons, a 28 year old black man, shot and
killed by Los Angeles County Sheriff deputies. Killed in front
of his family during a barbecue at Watts' Willowbrook Park.

Kenneth Hamilton, a 33 year old mentally disturbed
black man, shot and killed by Los Angeles Angeles County
Sheriff deputies responding to a call about a domestic dispute.
Accused of reaching for a pocket knife and shot 8 times in the
back while he lay face down on the ground.

Oliver Beasley, a 27 year old black man, shot to death
by Los Angeles County Sheriff deputies following a traffic
stop.

With the exception of the Compton Police officer,

whose first trail resulted in a hung jury for the murders of Pouvi Tualaulelei and Itali Tualaulelei, no criminal charges against the officers involved in the killing of these men and women were ever filed.

The residents of South-Central Los Angeles also remember Operation Hammer, a controversial Los Angeles police department operation that authorized and encouraged officers to indiscriminately stop minority youths. They remember the April, 1988, news interview with a Los Angeles police official who spoke enthusiastically about Operation Hammer saying, "Tonight, we pick'em up for anything and everything," and the resulting two-year harassment of their sons and daughters. By 1990, over 50,000 young people, primarily black and Hispanic young men had been arrested, harassed, and degraded. They'd been handcuffed, had guns pointed in their faces, treated like animals and forced to lie down in the filth of Los Angeles' city streets. Few of them were ever charged with a crime. Guilty only of being black or Hispanic.

In August, 1988, some 88 Los Angeles policemen raided a group of apartments in the 3900 block of Dalton street in South-Central Los Angeles. After beating 32 residents with guns, batons, and flashlights, and destroying their personal property and their apartment building they found no evidence of the crack houses that they were looking for. No criminal charges were filed against any of the residents but their lives were forever altered, their homes destroyed.

The less vicious, but widely publicized cases of Jamall Wilkes, popular former Los Angeles Lakers professional basketball player who was handcuffed and dehumanized by Los Angeles Police officers because his automobile registration was, "about to expire." And, Joe Morgan, former Cincinnati Reds professional baseball player who was thrown to the ground and handcuffed by Los Angeles Police officers because, "He looked like a drug dealer."

This is the reality of black America.

A reality defined by those like former Los Angeles Police Chief Daryl Gates who, after several blacks had died as a result of the Los Angeles Police officers use of the controversial choke hold, without any remorse, commented that perhaps blacks were more vulnerable *"than normal people."* One of a long list of well publicized racist stereotypes made of the Los Angeles minority community.

A reality defined by the Christopher Commission which published a report describing the racist, sexist, brutal police culture that existed in the Los Angeles Police Department. The report spoke of a black policemen who told of his concern of being stopped and harassed by fellow officers after late duty, simply because he was black. The report told of a Los Angeles Police Department which provided an environment where officers used excessive force with impunity. Where accountability within the department was non-existent. The report outlined the openly racist, sexist, and documented communications of Los Angeles Police officers subsequent to, and following the Rodney King beating.

Our reality has been defined by the graphic photographs and videotapes of police dogs savagely biting people who had been charged with no crimes, who simply were black or brown, homeless and too helpless to do anything. We heard the stories of policemen who laughed while their dogs inflicted such pain and suffering. Who rewarded their dogs by allowing them to bite citizens of this country who, in many cases had not even been suspected of a crime.

Our community witnessed the January, 1992, release of two black men, having served 17 years of a life sentence, for a murder that they had been convicted of committing as a result of falsified evidence, coerced and perjured testimony by Los Angeles Police officers. For seventeen years these two men were forced into a brutal, racist cage by policemen who lived above the law. Their lives and the lives of their families permanently altered by a blatantly racist judicial system seldom concerned with truth and rarely interested in justice when it comes to the rights and lives of minorities in America. A judicial system where white men play Russian roulette with the lives of our husbands and wives, fathers and mothers, sons and daughters. For them it's a well-paid game that they play for personal gratification and financial gain. For us, the judicial system is our worse nightmare. A twilight zone where money, power, and perceptions control our destiny. Not truth. Not evidence. Not justice.

Our reality has been shaped by the killing of Latasha Harlins, a black teenager, shot by a Korean store owner as she walked away after an argument over a $1.79 bottle of orange juice. As she approached the counter to pay the store owner accused her of trying to steal the orange juice. The subsequent argument and the shooting, as captured on videotape, showed the store owner first arguing with the teenager and then shooting the teenager in the back of the head as she turned to leave the store. Following a manslaughter conviction, a white judge sentenced the store owner to probation. Prior to this sentencing, a black mailman had been sentenced to six months in jail for shooting a dog and another black man had been sentenced to 30 days in jail for kicking a dog.

Our reality tells us that kicking a dog will get you more time in jail than killing our children.

Chapter 2

A boiling rage

It's been said that when America catches a cold, black America catches pneumonia. The 1991 recession was felt throughout the entire fabric of American society. Some of the wealthiest individuals and nation's largest businesses were forced into bankruptcy. From New York's Park Avenue to California's Beverly Hills, many among the rich and famous have fallen. Foreclosed property, repossessed automobiles, IRS tax liens, and securities and investments fraud leading to criminal prosecutions and civil suits have touched many in America's inner circle of wealth and power.

Over nine million Americans from every social, economic, professional and educational level have filed for unemployment compensation. From IBM to General Motors, from the mail room to the board room, from MBAs to Ph.Ds. The best, the brightest, the most experienced, and those who thought their employment safe and secure have found themselves in the same unemployment lines and asking the same questions as the disadvantaged and displaced. However, they will find no sympathy from those who have been stuck at the bottom. Those who have been unable to escape America's urban jungles because of political patronage and corporate nepotism which awards thousands of jobs annually to friends, family, friends of friends, and friends of family. They have no sympathy for the human resource specialists who reject employment applications because those applying live in such urban communities as Watts, Compton, and South-Central Los Angeles.

A new battle wages as minorities, who are often lacking in education and experience, who, historically have been relegated to limited employment opportunities now find themselves with even more limited access to employment as displaced white and blue collar workers compete for those same jobs.

As unemployment in America climbed over 7%, unemployment in inner-city communities exceeded 50%, with black and Latino youth leading the way with over 75% unemployment. There are simply too few opportunities for those stuck in urban America with little education, few skills, and little on the job experience. With displaced college educated professionals seeking the dwindling number of entry level jobs which they too have sought as store clerks, secretaries, mail handlers, and customer service representatives what are they to do? The systematic dismantling of federal job training and assistance programs has left young blacks and Hispanics frustrated and without direction. They have few options and little hope.

Public education in our urban communities is failing America. Administrators who want to develop programs that effectively teach all children are trapped by policies and politics. They are unable to implement effective programs to reward good teachers and to get rid of bad ones. There are too many teachers who dislike our children and despise parents and administrators who expect them to do their job, "teach our children!" I've seen them in my workshops. They bring their knitting, magazines, and newspapers. They sit there because they're paid to be there. They sit near those who share their dislike of our children and laugh and whisper among themselves. They're not interested in effective teaching strategies. They're not interested in new ideas that could possibly turn the tide of miseducation and *noneducation* of our children. They are quick to blame the parents, many of whom themselves were miseducated by similar uncaring teachers. They are quick to blame the administration, lack of materials, overcrowded classrooms, and apathy among their students. They label our children and program them to fail through lowered expectations, negative language, and their insensitivity to the unique stresses and problems of children in urban communities. They are liars and hypocrites who destroy the dreams of our children. They should have a special interest in the nightly newscasts which tell us each night of the young black and brown children dying in America's urban battlefields. Being gunned down by children, many whom had their self-esteem destroyed by the negative comments of uncaring teachers. Children who had their dreams crushed by teachers who told them that their dreams and aspirations were unrealistic or who implied through their actions or language that they were dumb and limited in their potential. There are simply too many in public education who are destroying the public whom they are being paid to educate.

And yet, what of the teachers who want to educate our children. Teachers who must do battle daily with negative and insensitive teachers and administrators. Teachers who are being placed into combat duty in schools which are unsafe, classrooms which are overcrowded, and find books and supplies nonexistent. Teachers who are responsible for educating our children and shaping the future of America are being paid less than those responsible for collecting our trash. It's an embarrassment. We can spend billions of dollars on weapons and space exploration but we cannot provide the support for good teachers who are teaching and the incentives for good people who want to teach? Teachers too often are finding themselves on a battlefield with gang bangers and drug dealers in their hallways, on the playground, and controlling the streets of their communities threatening their lives and the lives of those who wish to learn.

Many of our children, our teachers, our administrators, and our communities have simply given up on public education. At many of our schools administrators, teachers, and students alike simply come to put in their time. Yet, our children become angry and frustrated when they discover that public education has ill-prepared them for college admission. Even if they could qualify for college admission, few have found the necessary resources to pay college tuition. If they are among the dwindling number who graduate from inner-city high schools they find that a high school diploma prepares them for little in this society. Not even the most basic employment, which in itself can hardly be found. Thus, they are trapped in a community of few jobs and little opportunity.

Young blacks who have survived the battleground of urban America find themselves in a new battle in college confronting an increasing hostile and overtly racist atmosphere as more whites and other minorities are competing for the scarcely available financial resources. They find themselves being forced to justify their right to attend majority colleges and universities in face of the American perception that all blacks are riding on the magic carpet of affirmative action and are somehow depriving more deserving whites. Thus, young blacks are beginning to react to the increase in racially motivated hate crimes. They are becoming increasingly angry at their perception that the American government's preoccupation with the cries from other segments of the society has caused it to less vigorously pursue civil rights violations, constitutional enforcement, and the prosecution of cases resulting from racism, sexism, and bigotry.

As people watching the explosion within Los Angeles, and throughout the country, ask the naive question, "Why are these people so upset." As President Bush, in his state of the union address, perpetuated this naive vision of reality when he focused on using brute force to restore order to Los Angeles without providing the moral leadership in acknowledging to the American people that there is something desperately wrong in America.

The disgust that President Bush expressed publicly after watching unemployed, poor, and frustrated people take clothes, televisions, and groceries from stores compares little to the disgust and distrust that these people have in our government and in America's affluent. An affluent who, despite appearing to have everything, stole millions of dollars through HUD, savings and loans, insurance companies, and investment companies.

South-Central Los Angeles represents a microcosm of America's underclass who have seen the highly publicized reports of CEO's of companies cut jobs while they receive hundreds of thousands of dollars in pay raises and bonuses. A Congress, who, year after year remains impotent in enacting legislation to educate and provide incentive for investment in urban America while they vote themselves pay raises and lavishly spend our money on themselves and their staffs. They freely wrote bad checks while those whom they represent in urban America paid a premium to cash their miniscule welfare and social security checks at check cashing outlets and liquor stores. We have seen the televised stories of Government officials who had their staffs do their grocery shopping, who spent millions of dollars flying government aircraft and riding in limousines, whose children are educated in private schools, whose lives are filled with the frills and conveniences equaled only by *Lifestyles of the Rich and Famous*.

Those trapped in urban America, while not understanding macro and micro economic theories know that the conscience of this country is swayed by powerful lobbyist and campaign contributors. That justice in America is not blind and to the contrary is a perversion of power, money, and racism. Hopelessly frustrated they are angry that America isn't listening to them. America isn't interested in their pain. They exist at the very bottom of our socioeconomic ladder, unemployed and unemployable, unskilled and ill-prepared to plan a way out of their despair yet we expect them to do better for themselves.

The black and minority community has become increasingly vocal and angry in its opposition to police brutality, to the inability of our public schools to effectively educate our children, and to the apparent inability of our tax dollars to find their way back into our communities. We are tired of the institutional racism in the banking industry that denies us equal access to personal credit, business loans, and home mortgages. Of red-lining in the insurance industry that denies us equal access and comparable premiums for automobile and business insurance. We are angry and frustrated that through it all we are forced to fight a continuing battle for basic civil liberties guaranteed by the constitution upon which this country was founded.

Young blacks particularly, in increasingly growing numbers have adopted the radical and revolutionary philosophies and ideologies articulated by a young Malcolm X. They are being pumped up by rap music whose energy, beat, videos, and lyrics speak to their pain and anger offering violence as their solution. Rap artists, who, like the Piped Piper play their music to which children, black, white, and brown march hypnotically. Those rap artists who preach education and personal responsibility are overshadowed by the media attention given those who rap about sex and violence. Unfortunately it is they who stomp around on the stages of America preaching violence and feeding off of the feelings of frustration, hopelessness, and powerlessness of our children. The violence in Los Angeles, Atlanta, San Francisco, Seattle, and in communities throughout the country following the acquittal of the officers in the Rodney King case was certain to happen.

America had turned a deaf hear to their pain, anger, frustration, and feelings of hopelessness. The victims had become the problem. The underclass had become the unwelcome. One of the jurors echoed America's lack of understanding with her comments, "They just needed an excuse to commit violence." In her mind it had nothing to do with the Rodney King case. In her reality civilize people in our society don't behave like the policemen who beat Rodney King. Nor do they behave like the people across America who took to the streets following the verdicts. Thus, in her mind the conduct of the policemen was acceptable, or at least not criminal, because it was the uncivilized behavior of Rodney King who drove them to do it. However, the conduct of those who took their frustrations into the streets of America is unacceptable, criminal, and uncivilized, because in her reality they were uncivilized to begin with!

President Bush spoke harshly against the violence that exploded in the streets of America. He spoke of restoring order, not of restoring jobs. He spoke of their disgusting behavior, not of a system that has created and perpetuated the disgusting conditions in which they live. He spoke of having faith in our system of justice, not of removing the cancer of racism that plagues it. He spoke of coordinating federal troops to reclaim the streets of Los Angeles, not of coordinating federal support for the rebuilding of America's inner cities. He spoke of the justice department vigorously pursuing the Rodney King case, not of the vigorous pursuit of the thousands of victims brutalized by police throughout America whose stories were not captured on videotape. His comments sadly indicated that in his reality he had no conception of what drove them to do it.

Chapter 3

The explosion

On Wednesday, April 29, 1992, nearly a year from the date that the brutal beating of a black man, by three white Los Angeles police officers, was captured on videotape; a jury in the predominately white suburban community of Simi Valley California found two of the three officers who actually did the beating, together with a Sergeant who did nothing to stop the beating, not guilty of all charges. The jury was unable to reach a verdict on the charge of using excessive force by one officer.

For nearly a year this case was placed before the eyes of the world. Throughout the world as people watched the videotape they thought the scene more appropriately representative of an event in South Africa than in America. For many watching the tape in this country the scene would have been more appropriately placed in Alabama or Mississippi, certainly not in Los Angeles. Nearly everyone watching the videotape had found the behavior of those officers sickening and barbaric. These were clearly criminals functioning with impunity under the color of authority. Perhaps the apartheid system in South Africa would tolerate this. Perhaps corrupt third world governments and their gestapo like police forces would tolerate this. However, not in America. Not in the country which espouses rhetoric through its foreign policy on the world stage for democracy and human rights. Not the country which directed billions of dollars in military resources and other aid under the auspices of peace and human rights around the world.

Although the viciousness and brutality of the officers involved shocked the world and became a foreign policy embarrassment for America it placed before the eyes of the world what blacks and other minorities have been saying for years. The videotape traumatized many in Los Angeles, black and white alike. Whites began to view police stops, over minor traffic violations, with the same sense of fear and apprehension which we in the minority community have felt for years. Yet while this new reality was being experienced by people throughout the world. What about those in Simi Valley?

The verdicts were broadcast live. Sitting in my living room, over two thousand miles from Los Angeles, I listened as each verdict was read. With each not guilty verdict I cringed. As the final verdict was read, along with many throughout the world, I sat stunned. Wondering how, after the entire world had seen the videotape over and over, the case could end this way.

I sat in my living room and stared out of the window into the northern suburb of Atlanta's exclusive north side. An area of half million dollar homes, in beautiful private communities where both blacks and whites have come to settle away from the hustle, bustle, hopelessness, and despair of America's inner cities. I came here for the serenity to write and raise a family. Like so many other blacks, I left Los Angeles for a quiet, slower, more comfortable lifestyle.

In my work I speak to thousands of parents, teachers, and students throughout the country in such urban school districts as Los Angeles, San Francisco, Compton, Oakland, Detroit, Indianapolis, and Dallas. Through working with parents and teachers I understand the mounting frustration they experience raising and teaching young people who have lost faith in public education and accessibility to opportunities in America. Through working with young elementary, high school, and college students I know the pain, frustration, and rage that threatens to destroy their young lives.

As I stared out of my window I knew that an explosion was imminent. Less than an hour later the volcano would erupt. In South-Central Los Angeles on 71st and Normandie angry young men, together with residents of the community, would begin to rebel against the Los Angeles police and a society which had abandoned them. As the anger and frustration exploded so did the size of the crowd. In what would prove symbolic of how America responds to the crisis of urban America the Los Angeles police were ordered to leave the area. Unlike middle and upper class communities where officers are held responsible for protecting the lives and property of American citizens, urban America is allowed to destroy itself.

Without police intervention or rational leadership the anger and frustration of an enraged community erupts into an unforgiving and uncontrollable rage. Gang members who had previously terrorized the community lead the crowds to the intersection of Florence and Normandie where they terrorize and destroy property and lives as Los Angeles police officers continue to drive by. Urban America has been abandoned, left in the hands of young men who have been lost and forgotten. We had not taught them how to channel their enormous energy into bringing about real change. We had not helped them to develop true leadership skills. America had abandoned them as the Los Angeles police had abandoned their community.

The violent behavior of those who pulled people from their cars was frightening. The violence perpetuated against the entire community was irrational. While many sought to simply blame those involved for their behavior. Others saw a parallel between the young men who beat Reginald Denny, a white truck driver, and the officers who beat Rodney King.

Somehow attempting to justify one by the other. What I saw was a society which could not escape its responsibility in both. A police department which contributed to the culture of racism and brutality of its officers. And an American political, judicial, and public education system which contributed to the anger and brutality of the young men who beat Reginald Denny.

Many will make the argument that it is not the responsibility of public education to teach character and morality yet it is in public education that the dreams of young men like those terrorizing the streets of South-Central have been destroyed. Public education which too often fails to motivate or to inspire them into believing that there are opportunities for them in America.

As the first news reports came in I thought about the young people with whom I had spent a day just two weeks prior at the Washington Preparatory High School in South-Central Los Angeles. We spent the day building dreams. Most of them were high school seniors who were experiencing, for the first time in their lives, being encouraged to share their dreams. To speak of their dreams while those around them shouted, "You have the power to do that!" For a brief moment the frustration and hopelessness of their lives was being replaced with inspiration and aspiration. For the first time it was not only their time to dream but they were identifying and discussing the steps necessary to turn their dreams into reality. We weren't just daydreaming about our journey to the stars but planning to build the Space Shuttle that would take us there. Their dreams were becoming real. Not pie in the sky wishes, but goals that they had the power to achieve.

Young people who had come into the room lacking self-esteem and self-confidence. Who were simply coming to school and going through the motions. Sailing on ships with no clear destinations, inadequately supplied and under manned. Young black and Hispanic youths who were about to graduate from high school with no dreams, no job prospects, unrealistic expectations, and no resources to pursue a college degree. They came in sloppily dressed, angry, intimidating and projecting outward arrogance that shielded their lack of inner confidence. They felt put upon for being forced to be there. Some of them flat out told me that they weren't interested in what I had to say. They were tired of those who journey into America's forgotten and abandoned urban ghettos with hollow pep talks and programs that don't work. They were tired of the young black professionals who come to them to talk about their good jobs and important careers yet who fail to become their much needed mentors. They were tired of the band-aids that America continues to place upon the cancer that is killing their communities and at that moment, even before I had spoken a single word, they were tired of me.

I spoke to them in truth and in love. I was living the American dream, while they had no dreams to live. I was already looking twenty years into the future, while they weren't even looking forward to the next day. I hadn't come to lecture, or to plead, or to guaranty them any opportunity. I had come to work with whomever wanted to work. If you had a dream I would help you to develop a plan. If you didn't have a dream I would help you to define one. With the power and authority that God gives me I spoke to them. Finally, they had the option. They could sit where they were and complain about the injustices and oppression of America or they could join me on the other side of the room and we would work together to develop strategies to overcome the inevitable obstacles that confronted them.

As they looked around to see who would have the courage to join me the 6' 9" 250 lb. young man who had told me that he didn't want to hear anything that I had to say stood up and smiled. They all joined me on the other side of the room as we began building dreams. In the beginning none of them had wanted to be there now none of them wanted to leave. For the first time, it was their time. It was time to believe in them and to develop a plan of action for achieving their dreams. It was time for a new reality.

I thought about the young people at Bret Harte Middle School, John Muir Jr. High, and Forshay Jr. High. Other young people whom I had helped to build dreams. What were they doing now?

Had they taken to the streets? Had they forgotten the vision, and the new reality that we had developed for their lives? Within hours of the verdicts the city of Los Angeles and many of its surrounding communities had exploded. I spoke to friends who were attending the Los Angeles Lakers-Portland Trail Blazers NBA playoff game the night of the verdicts. They told me of leaving the game and driving through the streets and the frightening experience of driving through a war zone of police sirens, gun shots, fires, and electrical blackouts.

How did the explosion, which so many of us from the black community expected, catch so many of those in positions of power and leadership throughout America by surprise? Perhaps when people lay dormant and docile for so long you come to believe that they will accept just about anything. That their senses have become so dulled by the injustices leveled against them that virtually any injustice against them, if given in sufficiently small doses, will be tolerated. Perhaps there will be some whining and complaining, some moaning and groaning but certainly no violent reaction.

However, what happened in Los Angeles, and quickly spread throughout the country, was a violently uncontrollable reaction to a virus being introduced into the body of urban America. The injustice could have predictably exaggerated the sickening stomach ache, but even the patient was over-whelmed at the violent convulsions that resulted. President Bush, the Simi Valley jurors, the Los Angeles Police Department, all represented a system of racism, oppression, and injustice in America that had finally caused urban America to throw-up.

Many of those caught in the middle of the explosion had started out in angry, but peaceful demonstrations. The demonstration in Atlanta began as a bipartisan, multi-ethnic protest of this miscarriage of justice. However, the anger and frustration of the minority community had reached a boiling point and thus the rebellion against those who represented the oppressors.

While many whites were protesting the injustice, their reality was of the police beating a man and not being punished for their conduct. The reality of the minority community in general and blacks in particular was much broader. The policemen represented the system of racism, oppression and injustice of white America. A system validated by the nearly all-white Simi Valley jury and sanctioned by President Bush's ridiculous comments that the verdicts were wrong but that our system of justice was fair. The ensuing violence and brutality indiscriminately directed at all whites was wrong. But it was a brutal and violent reflection of racism in America. A racist attitude and ingrain perception of blacks and minorities that places us in a dangerously precarious position whenever we have to interface with authority in America. Whether in the criminal justice system, with policemen, in business, applying for employment, or in our dealings with state, local, and federal government too many of those who exercise power, control, and authority over our lives are white and racist.

In Atlanta, the anger was directed at those whites who were involved in the demonstration and others who simply got in the way. In Los Angeles the anger was directed at whatever whites happened to be in the way as well as white-owned and Asian-owned businesses operating within the black and Hispanic community. In the Los Angeles Crenshaw District large groups of angry and frustrated people walked down the street destroying all identifiable non-black-owned or Hispanic-owned businesses. Business after business along Crenshaw boulevard from nail salons to liquor stores, from grocery stores to dry cleaners were destroyed.

The Mayor of the City of Compton went on the radio to plead for the people to stop the burning and looting as they walked through the streets shouting, "No justice, no peace." Unlike the Watts riots of 1965, which were localized in the minority community, this anger touched communities all over Los Angeles County. As the television cameras broadcast the story throughout the world the angry faces were not just black, but white, yellow, and brown skin people who were fed up with the injustice and oppression that threatens to destroy America.

The violence caught everyone off guard. The Los Angeles law enforcement agencies were ill-prepared to deal with the public outrage. The California National Guard was unprepared for immediate deployment. Non-black or Hispanic-owned businesses throughout the black and Hispanic communities were unprepared for the rage that was forthcoming. The ongoing tension between the black community and the Korean community would become part of the explosion. The clash of cultures and realities provided more kindling for the fire. Within the reality of urban blacks burned a simmering rage toward Korean merchants for the years of disrespect, high prices, inferior products, and failure to become a part of the community and provide jobs for their children.

Angry people marched through the streets of Los Angeles, frustrated and enraged voices shouted, "Not this one, but burn that one."

No justice, no peace.

Chapter 4

Our children are searching

Police brutality cases involving Los Angeles policemen and Los Angeles County sheriff deputies have resulted in the physical abuse and death of blacks and other minorities for years. Although many have resulted in millions of dollars in civil judgements against the city and the law enforcement agencies involved, few have resulted in successful criminal prosecution with severe criminal penalties against the officers who have cruelly caused death or other physical abuse under the color of authority. Why would a not guilty verdict in this particular case be any different? After all, nearly a year had passed since the beating.

Undoubtedly many discussions, expert analysis, and socioeconomic theories will attempt to explain what happened. Those who don't understand the pain of urban america will attempt to blame single-parent families, lack of family values, or unemployment as the root causes of the explosion. However, those who I have spoken to in South-Central Los Angeles say it was the videotapes. The tape of Latasha Harlins, a black teenager, shot in the head over orange juice. The tape of Don Jackson, a black former Hawthorne Police Sergeant who has been on a crusade to expose police brutality, whose face was shown being shoved through a store window following a traffic stop by Long Beach Police officers. And, the year-long showing of the Rodney King videotape kept the images before the eyes and in the minds of the black community.

And, the expectations.

Blacks, both middle class and lower class, most whites, and most of those viewing the videotape throughout the world knew that the officers were guilty. The videotape provided indisputable evidence of the unprovoked violence that took another human being to within a thread of death. Those involved had no respect for his life, their reality did not allow them to identify with his pain. To the black community the videotape came to symbolize years of injustice and brutality. The world could finally see that we have not been exaggerating in our claims that there is one standard for white America and a different one for black America.

The videotape had awakened the consciousness of America. The reality of America had been exposed to the pain of blacks and other minorities. America was ready to make these four officers (the three who did the beating and the Sergeant who did nothing to stop it) an example that this type of conduct would no longer be tolerated in this country. America would finally awaken to the cries of the many thousands of people throughout the country who have been reporting cases of police brutality pleading for justice. Frustrated by investigators, district attorneys, judges, and juries they have found the system stacked against them. Even when they receive huge civil settlements as compensation for the brutality leveled against them there is anger that the policemen continue in many cases to go unpunished by our courts and without serious reprimands by their departments. For many the expectations were high, the disappointment profound. The volcano erupted and America is hurting.

*   *   *

Black high school and college students are angry that over a hundred years after the Emancipation Proclamation blacks in America are still fighting for equal human respect in this society. That nearly three decades after the passage of the Civil Rights Act of 1964, the brutal beatings and vicious shootings of blacks by law enforcement officers throughout America continues. The videotaped beating of Rodney King, together with the subsequent acquittal of the officers involved, evoked the images of overt racism, lynching, and the sanctioned and legitimized killing of black men and women throughout the history of this country.

Children in minority communities throughout the country, particularly black and Latino males who are falling victim to homicide and entering American prisons at an overwhelming disproportionate rate in terms of their percentage of the general population, have lost faith in the idea of equality and fairness in the judicial system in America. Disregarded and abandoned they are mad at America. Their reality has been shaped by the facts that their communities appear powerless to improve their schools. That they remain unemployed with no skills and no direction. Surrounded by hopelessness and frustration they feel an overwhelming negative and chronically depressing sense of helplessness. From their graffiti to their gangs they mark their turf and were their colors and are willing to die for the vacant lots and street corners that they claim ownership of. They have no dreams as all of the slices of the American pie have been taken by others leaving them with only the empty and unwanted pie pan.

They feel helpless to uplift themselves from the desperation and despair of their communities. They feel powerless to speak out when they are the victims of police harassment and brutality. They feel that there is no one who will lobby on their behalf. No one who will listen to their cries. No one who can protect them from the gangs, drugs, and violence which has turned the streets of urban America into Beirut like battle fields.

They are questioning why we were able to spend billions of dollars and effectively coordinate the movement of thousands of pieces of military equipment and personnel half way around the world to fight for the freedom of Kuwait and Panama. Yet, we as a nation have been continually ineffective at providing safe communities, job training programs, business opportunities, jobs and health care for them and their families. Why doesn't America have the will to direct the energy and resources to free them from the hopelessness and despair of urban America?

The new reality that is emerging from the aftermath of Los Angeles provides a frightening prophecy for America. Urban America has witnessed the outpouring of federal aid and corporate sponsorship to rebuild businesses and the community following the violence and destruction. The aftermath brings new hope to those in South-Central. The energy, attention, and resources being directed towards their problems suggests that America will only respond to their pain when a revolution is imminent. How will this new reality affect such urban communities as Chicago, New York, Detroit, Atlanta, Miami, Philadelphia, and Washington, D.C?

The unfortunate reality shared by so many middle and upper class Americans is that the people in South-Central Los Angeles, and in hundreds of communities like it throughout the country, don't want to do better for themselves. That the mothers and fathers who feel powerless to change their situations don't want to see better for their children. Teachers across America, with whom I have worked share this reality. They believe that black boys and Hispanic boys are inherently bad. That their behavior is inherently criminal and destructive, and that most of them have no real chance of succeeding in

America. They believe they will all become gang members, drug dealers, or go to prison. They are labeling and programming our children to fail through lowered expectations, school suspensions, culturally biased testing, and ability tracking.

Our children have come to feel unwanted and inferior as the result of the subtle and even overtly racist ways in which they are treated in stores, in classrooms, in restaurants, riding public transportation, and in their encounters with law enforcement.

They are our children, who are saying to us by their actions and through the looks of frustration on their faces, as we rush off in pursuit of the American Dream, what about us? As America allocates its time, scarce resources, and energy fighting battles for freedom around the world, what about us? As the Federal Government allocates billions of dollars for bailing out the savings and loan industry, what about our schools? As American industry moves its manufacturing facilities from our urban communities to rural America or out of America altogether, where will we work? As American public education continues to fail large numbers of minority youth, ill-preparing them for college, ill-preparing them for occupational jobs after high school, and ill-preparing them for entrepreneurship, they are asking what are we to do?

How can our children understand that we as a nation are willing to spend more money to keep them in prison for the rest of their lives than we are to educate and prepare them to become valuable, productive, contributing members of this society? How can they understand a society that is willing to pay millions of dollars to keep them from selling drugs but little to provide them with real employment and entrepreneurial opportunities. A society willing to spend billions of dollars on space exploration but little on community programs and job training, or to protect them from the gangs, abusive households and law enforcement officials which threaten to destroy their lives? Our children have more questions than we have answers. For too many of them their reality offers little hope of a brighter tomorrow. For too many of us our reality doesn't allow us to understand their pain.

*   *   *

Not long ago, my wife and I drove through downtown Los Angeles where we saw hundreds of homeless people along the streets. Many of them were so dirty you couldn't tell where the dirt ended and their clothes began. My wife, shook her head and said, "How can people live like this? Why won't they do something for themselves?"

Her comments brought back childhood memories of growing up on Chicago's South Side and the black men who stood each day on street corners, lost and hopeless, their spirits broken and defeated. They had given up fighting and had resolved within their souls that they had no power to change their situations. Without an understanding of their realty few of us can understand the hopelessness and despair that has consumed their lives. This is why I understand the children who are searching for leaders. Leaders who will give them a brighter vision. Who will give them hope for the future. Leaders who will make the little black and Latino boys and girls believe that they are important and that their lives are as valuable as those of little white boys and girls.

The jurors who acquitted the officers in the beating of Rodney King, the judge who sentenced the Korean store owner to probation in the killing of Latasha Harlins, the jurors who found no basis for criminal charges against the police officers and sheriff deputies in the killings of Oliver Beasley, Arturo Jiminez, Steven Clemons, and Kenneth Hamilton, cannot see the reality of the brutalization of our children. That's why they cannot understand the rage.

Chapter 5
What must our leaders do?

Those in America who set the political, social, moral, and spiritual agenda of the nation through their action and/or inaction set the tone of acceptable conduct for the nation. Beginning with the President of the United States, right down to our local city council and school board members, through their actions and/or inaction, through their language and position on the social, and moral issues of our nation and our communities, they set a national tone. President Bush and his military advisors drew a well publicized "line in the sand" over which we went to war with Sadaam Hussaan. As a nation we were willing to sacrifice the lives of men and women, mothers and fathers, together with billions of dollars over a line in the sand.

But what of the lines between justice and injustice, racism and American citizenry, sexism and human dignity, fairness and unfairness, equality and inequality, and black and white which divides this country. The line that allows the police department in Beverly Hills the staff, equipment, technology, and training to provide disproportionately better service and responsiveness to its citizens than the Los Angeles police department and those assigned to urban communities like South-Central. The line that too often allows the best and brightest teachers and administrators in urban schools to be transferred to already superior suburban schools or trap them in dangerous urban schools with inadequate supplies and resources. The line that allows the federal, state, and local government to take the income and property tax dollars of urban communities without mandating the reinvestment of those dollars in effective programs to empower those communities.

The President of the United States has an undeniable and inextricable social and moral responsibility to the American people to mandate that the federal government, particularly the Justice Department, aggressively pursues any and all violations of the civil rights of all of our citizens. A mandate which ensures that the words "One nation under God, indivisible, with liberty and justice for all," is a pledge which becomes embodied within the spirit of everyone who serves within the system of government in America. This is the leadership that sends a clear and uncompromising message to state and local governments and law enforcement agencies that American citizenship has value and that equal justice under the law is uncompromising. That the human and civil rights of American citizens becomes a line in the sand over which others cannot cross. A mandate that the elected and non-elected officials throughout every branch of government aggressively pursue racism, sexism, bigotry, and injustice in America. This is the leadership that sets a moral tone that our nation will not tolerate injustice on any level.

There is an even greater responsibility among the clergy who preach religion on Saturday and Sunday while burying their heads in the sand when aware of the racism, sexism, and injustice practiced by their congregations and their communities. Those who profess to be called by God cannot refuse to put on the whole armor of God and take an uncompromising stand for justice. The Pastors and Priests of churches whose buildings stand in suburban or privileged communities must stand up against the wrongdoings of the executives, politicians, criminals and racists who come to church on Sunday asking forgiveness for their sins against humanity throughout the week. The Pastors and Priests of churches whose buildings stand in urban communities cannot refuse to stand up against the injustice and inequality directed at their communities. The clergy cannot simply take in tithes and offerings as a furtherance of God's message and ignore the moral injustice that exists around them.

It is the white clergy particularly who must step to the forefront accepting the spiritual and moral leadership in preaching an end to the racism, sexism, bigotry, and injustice perpetuated by those in their congregations throughout this society.

The black clergy, from which emerged our most celebrated civil rights leaders, must take a strong and uncompromising stand against injustice in this society. Together, they must set a spiritual agenda that those who walk with God cannot perpetuate the systematic and institutionalized hatred and injustice which are destroying America. It is they who cannot disavow their responsibility in bringing about the spiritual awakening needed to build the bridge of tolerance and understanding between urban despair and suburban prosperity, between the social elite and the urban abandoned, between those who are living their dreams and those who have no dreams to live.

In locker rooms and board rooms, in country clubs, and at social gatherings where the racist jokes are being told, people must become empowered with the spiritual and moral courage to speak out. Banks continue to unfairly deny loan applications for personal, mortgage, and business loans by blacks as a result of racist and biased underwriters and lending officers. Someone in the bank knows who they are and that what they're doing is wrong. In businesses where blacks, women, and other minorities, no matter how qualified, are consistently downgraded in their performances and continue to receive the lowest pay increases, whites who say that they aren't racist or sexist condone through their inaction those who perpetuate a system of institutionalized racism and sexual bias. Churches must set the spiritual tone that deplores such conduct as unacceptable in the church and destructive to America.

The code of silence among police officers, which allows the continuing misconduct of racism, sexism, bigotry, and brutality, is contributing to the destruction of America. Few within this society cannot count a racist or bigot among their friends. We tolerate it because our friends are more important to us than the harm their attitudes inflict upon people whom we don't know. We tolerate it because we lack the courage to take a stand. We live in a reality where we feel that if we don't talk about it, we can remain safe in our little world and that the ugliness will not touch us. Our reality convinces us that if we don't deal with it, it will go away by itself. Unfortunately, it is that reality which perpetuates attitudes that allow racist, uncaring decisions to be made throughout the entire fabric of our society which affect all of our communities.

It is the lack of leadership from both the church and the state that perpetuated the attitudes which allowed the Los Angeles police department and Los Angeles County sheriff deputies to inflict pain, suffering, and daily indignities upon those trapped in our urban communities. It is that lack of leadership that has convinced too many of our children that gangs and crime are their only alternatives. And it is that lack of leadership which keeps suburban America out of touch with the reality of urban America.

*   *   *

America is in desperate need of individual consciousness raising as the pool of would be leaders lack morality and integrity. The politicians, televangelists, rappers, and gang bangers who capture front page headlines and dominate the nightly news with their press conferences and PR stunts. They claim to understand the pain of urban America as its self-appointed spokespersons.

The politicians journey into urban America, under armed guard and in the spotlight of television cameras. They speak of rebuilding the structures but not of rebuilding the dignity and self-respect that America has stripped from those trapped in our inner cities. They speak of job programs as a panacea for the urban poor. They naively believe that having a job will increase the self-image and self-worth of those who feel trapped in urban America while police continue to beat them over the head and public schools continue to ill-prepare them to develop a vision for their lives.

The televangelists pray for their pain and their prosperity as long as they skim a little from their welfare checks to support their multi-million television ministries and personal bank accounts.

The rappers take in millions of dollars from our children who are hypnotized and addicted to their music and lyrics of sex and violence. Children who are looking for solutions are being led by self-appointed leaders who set a code of language and dress that further separates our children from the institutions which control America. They offer our children violent solutions to their personal conflicts suggesting that they kill whites, policemen, their families, or anyone who stands in their way. Their lyrics degrade and dehumanize women of color while graphically portraying sexual conduct for our children who are already in a moral and spiritual struggle with teenage pregnancies, homicides, and rape.

Since the violence in Los Angeles, the media has been fascinated with the talk of young gang members who claim to have come together to rebuild. However, those of us who have lived the horror of urban America, where gang leaders have directed our young sons to kill each other as nothing more that an initiation rite, are not as quick to elevate these would be terrorists to would be community leaders. We are not so soon to forget how they have turned our communities into war zones where machine gun bullets indiscriminately leave our parents, elderly, and children lame or dead in our streets.

Aren't these the same young men whose fights over turf and colors have taken more lives in our communities than all of the wars in which we have fought? We are skeptical that those who have admittedly placed no value upon the lives of those outside their inner circle of homeys are now the media appointed spokespersons for urban America. After all, aren't these the same young men who have robbed our stores, broken into our homes, raped our wives and daughters, killed our children, terrorized our elderly, defaced every standing wall within their communities, and have held our communities hostage for years?

Although many have stepped forward to speak for the minority community following the violence, we must be leery of those who had not stepped forward before the violence. We are not in need of more leaders as much as we are in need of leadership from within.

If new leaders are to rise from the ashes of Los Angeles, they must do so from within the spirits of our children. But we must teach our children personal integrity and accountability. We must empower them with those inalienable qualities that build human character. Not only must these qualities be taught at home, they must become an integral part of the core curriculum taught our children in public education. Personal morality and spirituality are concepts that are rarely taught in our classrooms yet are essential to the spiritual and moral empowerment of urban America. And, while we refuse to empower public education with the charge of whole-child development, we continue to take the criminal products of an ineffective public education system and lock them up in an equally ineffective prison system. The reality of teachers convinces them that character, integrity, morality, spirituality, and human dignity must be taught at home. Yet, their reality must accept the fact the our educational system did not prepare parents for those responsibilities and does little to help parents develop those parenting skills today. The reality is that our children continue to walk an endless cycle through the revolving door of American public education and the American prison system.

Those who do not live in America's inner cities are inextricably tied to those who do. By creating another generation of hopelessly frustrated people who perceive little opportunity for themselves, we provide fertile ground for their feelings of abandonment, hostility, and alienation toward America. Their reality accepts crime and violence as their only means of survival. All of America becomes their victims either directly or indirectly. We become the victims of their brutal crimes or we pay for the *criminalization* process through our taxes and insurance premiums to pay for law enforcement, prisons, the courts, and insurance settlements. Those who do not turn to criminal activities still become the next generation of illiterate, powerless, and abusive parents.

No matter where we live, we cannot escape the responsibility of investing in urban America through professional training and assistance, business opportunities and jobs, parent training, and the spiritual and moral development of our children. This is the reality that must be accepted by a nation which professes to be a great nation in order to send a signal to the world that we care about and are willing to shoulder the responsibility for helping all of America. But most importantly, those who have no cultural or ethnic ties to America's urban underclass must understand that where they live is on American soil, their public schools are American public schools, and their pain, suffering, and frustration, have become an American tragedy.

Our political leaders must stop talking about what they're going to do about education and invest in specific programs to develop the consciousness and character of our children. If we develop specific programs to teach practical job and vocational skills, college preparation courses, and entrepreneurship in our most embattled urban communities, then maybe our children will begin to develop a vision of opportunity for themselves and their communities. If our national and local leaders approach every allegation of police brutality, sexual harassment, and racial discrimination from the perspective that such conduct is inexcusable, unacceptable, and will in no way be tolerated by those in positions of leadership in our society, our urban communities will begin to feel that they too are American citizens. However, if the citizens of our country cannot achieve a level of confidence in the American system of justice and believe that it is reasonably fair and reasonably just, we will continue to be at risk of the violence that erupted throughout the country following the "not guilty" verdicts in the Rodney King police brutality case.

Chapter 6

A new reality

Many have watched the violence occurring throughout urban America with a sense of disbelief. They ask, "Why would people behave that way? Why would people destroy their own communities? Don't they realize that they are only hurting themselves?" These questions are frequently raised by people with reasoning and critical thinking skills, people who are able think through the correlation between one's actions and the multitude of possible repercussions. However, it is the ability to think in this way which gives people options. These thinking and reasoning skills allow people to look at their problems and scan the range of possible solutions. It was this thinking from which was born the American Revolution. The colonists, who wanted to be self-governed, reasoned that the most viable solution to achieve that end was revolution. However, what if the leaders of the American Revolution, who were among the privileged and educated, did not possess the critical thinking skills to arrive at such a solution? The anger and frustration which were outwardly directed toward Britain could have been inwardly directed toward self-destruction as in the case of urban America.

When working with teachers in inner-city schools, I try to help them understand the reality of the children and their parents who live in urban America. Understanding the pain, anger, hopelessness, and frustration of their reality is essential if we are to provide the leadership that gives them hope. Understanding their reality is imperative if jurors, like those in Simi Valley, from the isolated, predominately white communities of America are to render verdicts that attempt to administer justice to all Americans.

When teachers are able to see reality through the eyes of their students, only then can they begin to effectively communicate, develop teaching styles, and develop programs that help young people expand their vision of the possibilities for succeeding within this society.

Government, civic, and community leaders can never understand the frustration, mistrust, and rage that residents within our urban communities feel without seeing reality through their eyes. Spending more money, allocating more resources, and starting more programs will not in and of themselves ease tensions and renew hope within urban America. Too much money is spent and too many resources squandered on programs that have no chance of succeeding since these programs are often conceived without the involvement of those whom the programs are suppose to assist. Thus, the programs are tainted by the reality of those who don't know the pain, frustration, and rage consuming those in urban America.

Throughout Los Angeles County, people are dealing with the trauma of the violence based upon new or old realities. Those who hold onto their old realities simpy blame the people for the violence. They have no sympathy for their communities and no empathy for their plight. They simply want those who perpetuated the violence to be put into our already overcrowded jails. They want more policemen on the streets and those who commit crimes to be kept in jail indefinitely.

America must learn from the new reality of those

throughout Los Angeles County who have come to South-Central to rebuild. Those who are dealing with the trauma from a newly defined reality have come into South-Central to help in the clean-up effort. Many are experiencing urban America up close and in person for the first time. They have never been there before. As they hold brooms, dressed in t-shirts and jeans, with their hands, clothes, and faces sweating and dirty, they have, for the first time, connected with the pain of America's distant and forgotten underclass. As their new reality unfolds old perceptions explode. Churches bring in truckloads of food. Neighbors barbecue for those without gas or electricity. As they talk and listen to the old people and to the children they realize that these are Americans who have been living an American nightmare.

They begin to share, not through third party agencies, but in person. They stand face to face with those who feel themselves America's unwanted. Those whom we have condemned to a life of poverty and welfare, living in communities that have deteriorated into desperate and violent urban jungles not because America doesn't have the ability or resources but because America doesn't have the will.

They see the frustration, hopelessness, and despair on the faces of those who live here. The desensitizing that they've received from the television and newspapers has been replaced with the hands on, face to face, anguish that these are real people who daily endure a living hell.

They've sent truckloads of food, clothing, and love. They've embraced our children and our community with the love and compassion needed to end the cycle of hopelessness and despair. The movie stars and politicians, the professional athletes and businessmen, the community organizers and clergy, officials from Washington and officials from the California Governor's office have joined hands for the first time and work side by side to clean up and to rebuild. For the first time, those who drive through this community on their daily commute have stopped their cars. For the first time since 1965, America is focusing on its problems.

Chapter 7

What now?

Watching the videotaped beating of Rodney King and the subsequent beatings of whites and Koreans during the backlash following the not guilty verdicts of the officers charged in his beating provides for many a new perspective and a new reality. A reality that America is dangerously close to a race war. A war that is being encouraged by hate groups and white supremacy organizations whose rhetoric blames the victims for their own victimization feeding the fears of white America and perpetuating the stereotype of black America.

The polarization of America is being perpetuated by conservatives who take the position that America has done enough for its poor and that the poor must be left to do for themselves. And by politicians who cater to the fear of suburban America through their get tough on crime speeches which perpetuates the stereotype that crime and violence are inherently linked to blacks and other minorities. They are encouraging a war that our police, national guard, or armed forces will not be able to control. The anger that fueled the violence in Los Angeles, San Francisco, Atlanta, Seattle, New York, and cities throughout the country has taught us a valuable and painful lesson. Something is desperately wrong in

America.

Those who ignore the hate crimes since they are not its victims together with those who ignore the racist and bigoted jokes told at country clubs, in staff meetings, and at cocktail parties are condoning an attitude that is dangerous to America. Those who lock themselves behind closed doors making unfair, unethical, and immoral decisions in corporate America's board rooms, in city council chambers, in school board meetings, and in the state and federal Houses of Representatives are pushing America to its destruction. Those who allow zoning ordinances, red-lining, and inequitable and unfair treatment of minorities attempting to build viable businesses in, and take ownership of, their communities are destroying the infrastructure of America.

Blacks are angry that few of the businesses within our communities are black-owned and that most of them provide no employment opportunities for the people who live within the community. There has been a long history of cultural clashes with Asian business owners who have openly acknowledged their lack of respect toward black customers. Their reality perpetuates a stereotype that blacks are lazy and that they come into their stores to steal. Many stores sell inferior products at highly inflated prices to customers who are unwilling or unable to shop elsewhere. Poor blacks particularly feel powerless to demand higher quality products, lower prices, and more courteous service. It is these feelings of powerlessness that fuels their anger.

Blacks are also angry at the perception by lending institutions that blacks aren't capable of building stable, profitable businesses within our communities. Blacks continue to be denied access to capital through traditional lending sources and fail to implement the collective buying and lending strategies that the Korean community has successfully employed in opening businesses throughout urban communities. Many urban communities whose residents lack self-pride suffer from a chronically depressing lack of community pride. Self-pride and community pride evolves from experiencing success in personal achievement, in business and property ownership. The lack of self-pride and community pride continues to eat away at the spirit of urban America. As urban America deteriorates, the realities of America move further apart.

Middle and upper class black America cannot escape its responsibility to reconnect with those blacks trapped in urban America. No matter how far education and opportunity take us, we are inextricably ethnically and culturally connected. No matter how professionally successful or financially affluent we become, race conscious America will always remind us that we are black and that the best that we achieve will always be overshadowed by the worst that those in our community do.

Black America must wake-up to the realization that too many of us are too busy chasing the American dream, climbing corporate ladders, playing on the golf courses, and joining the country clubs of white America to join the battle against the problems that are causing urban America to explode. We talk about the injustices in the American judicial system, yet, many of us avoid jury duty. I know many blacks who have bragged about the excuses that they used to get out of serving on jury duty. Blacks who drive through urban communities and shake their heads at the broken down cars, boarded up store fronts, and dirty streets pitying but not helping the homeless and helpless who remain powerless to change the despair of their communities.

In both Los Angeles' elite black and white communities, we have turned our back on the dirty little problems of America's inner cities. We know about the insensitive and ineffective politicians. We know that the tax dollars received from urban America are not effectively applied to the problems of urban America. Yet we won't help those trapped in urban America to effectively organize their voting power. Too many don't vote, and too many of those who do don't have an effective understanding of our political system and how to make the system responsive to their needs.

Many of the most financially affluent blacks have no active involvement in the African-American church. They avail themselves only for the annual Easter trek. In South-Central Los Angeles, churches, like liquor stores, are on virtually every street corner, each offering those who stumble in refuge from their pain. Many in the black community have been turned off to the black church because of its seemingly ineffectiveness in dealing with the problems within the black community. However, the congregation of churches, like the citizens of America, expect those in churches and government offices to resolve our problems. We pay taxes to the government, and we pay tithes and offerings to our churches (at least some of us), and we expect our social responsibilities to end with our financial contributions. We cannot disregard our personal responsibility to make our churches, schools, and government work. Pastors serve their congregations, politicians serve the people who elect them. It is our responsibility to follow the work of our pastors and elected officials. We must applaud, support, and assist in their efforts if effective and speak out or remove them when their work, or lack there of, is ineffective.

As we in middle and upper class black America financially and intellectually rise, our spiritual connection with blacks trapped in urban America declines. Our new reality tells us that if we can pull ourselves up by our bootstraps, they can do the same for themselves. Our selective memory tells us that we got to where we are as a result of our own hard work, diligence, determination, and our own personal commitment to succeed. Tragically, we have developed a view of reality that tells us that those trapped in the communities of urban America are responsible for their condition and don't want to do better for themselves.

Have we forgotten the ancestors whose shoulders we stand on? Have we forgotten the slave trade and the millions who died during the middle passage? Have we forgotten the brutal and barbaric institution of slavery which sanctioned the selling off and destruction of our families, the castration and lynching of our men, the raping of our women, and the abuse of our children? Have we forgotten those who bravely stood before the water hoses and police dogs to march for our voting and civil rights? Have we forgotten the battles that even the most intellectually and financially capable among us continue to fight daily throughout the entire fabric of this society? Have we forgotten that it was only the strength, courage, bonding, and faith in God within our community that enabled our community to survive the atrocities leveled against it.

We cannot forget that although the disgusting, and socially repulsive "White only" signs have been removed from America's restaurants and rest rooms, they continue to symbolically hang over the doors of America's juries and corporate board rooms. Perhaps blacks trapped in urban America better understand the reality of America than those of us who have left.

If we don't empower the collective consciousness of America to take a stand for justice, we are doomed as a nation. Which will become the next community to explode? The wounds are deep and the anger will burn long after the fires in Los Angeles go out unless America wakes up from its different realities.

Chapter 8

The implications for America

A special commission has issued a report critical of the Los Angeles police department and the Mayor's office for their ineffective response to the violence that left 60 people dead, over three thousand injured, over a billion dollars in property damage, and over five thousand businesses damaged or destroyed, many of which had no insurance. The Korean community was estimated to have incurred over 400 million dollars in property damage, hundreds of their businesses were destroyed, and hard working people died trying to defend their property. Their only crime was in trying to pursue an American dream in a community that had been forgotten by America. The commission report, while helping state and local governments better prepare themselves for the explosions ahead, does little to comfort the families and communities of those beaten or killed in the violence.

America still doesn't get it. Congress took over six months to structure an urban aid bill which was vetoed by President Bush. Like previous bills, it only offered band-aids to the problems of urban America while filling the already bulging pockets of political action committees and government lobbyists. The same people who have profited from the pain of urban America will profit from the destruction in Los Angeles.

Despite those who died, the communities which were destroyed, and the families whose lives were forever altered, our government has conducted business and politics as usual.

Those caught up in the violence and looting are still angry, frustrated, and poor. With the loss of over 40,000 jobs, the explosion has only added to the already overburdened roles of the unemployed as the flames and violence destroyed or ran away businesses which provided the few existing jobs in the community. Urban schools continue to be a breeding ground for angry young men who are pushed out of classrooms, expelled from schools, and turned off to education. Politicians continue to live in the lap of luxury insulated from the despair of urban America. Urban America knows that effective programs would not take so long to implement if those in Congress had to live their daily misery. To develop an effective urban aid plan we must require those who serve in federal, local, and state government to leave their federal and state offices and live in the communities they serve. We must require them to walk as those who have elected them walk. To experience the same lack of services, police harassment, and daily threats of crime and violence. This will help to awaken politicians to the reality of urban America.

To prevent future explosions we must empower those in urban America to exercise influence and control over their destiny. This can only happen when we more effectively help them to develop the rational and critical thinking skills needed to develop solutions to their problems. We must develop a new generation of leaders and spokespersons from within the community through training in group dynamics and how to effectively work on committees and task forces. We must develop their leadership skills and teach them how to recruit a cross coalition of young and old, white and blue collar, and entrepreneurs and working people to work together in resolving the community's problems. We have wasted the extraordinary leadership skills of young people leading gangs and crime rings by not providing them with and supporting positive leadership opportunities. We must provide them with leadership opportunities that would raise self-esteem and self-image by placing them at the forefront of the exodus of their people out of urban bondage.

Expending so much time and energy in registering people to vote has no real effectiveness unless we empower them to hold those whom they elect responsible to the needs of the community and accountable for their actions while serving the community. They can only hold their federal, local, and state officials accountable when they are made aware of who is responsible for what, how to contact those responsible, how to better publicize their effectiveness and/or ineffectiveness, and how their community can channel their anger and energy into organized, effective protest.

All of our attention is directed at the presidential candidates while we ignore the responsibility of those elected to serve urban America. With the exception of Congress-woman Maxine Waters and State Senator Diane Watson, there was no noticeable leadership among elected officials in calming the anger or of offering viable alternatives to the violence for those trapped in South-Central Los Angeles.

In Atlanta, I witnessed the leadership of Mayor Maynard Jackson who not only publicly took a stand against the violence but who went to personally speak to the angry young black college students who chanted, "No justice, no peace."

Mayor Jackson met with them and outlined how to channel their energy and anger into the three B's, the ballot, the buck, and the book. He employed them to use their voting power to elect those who would serve the needs of their communities. He employed them to use their economic power to support the businesses and organizations that are responsive to the needs of their communities. He told them to increase their quest for knowledge and the seriousness in which they approached their education. He explained that knowledge was the key to developing the strategies and solutions that would empower their communities. This was the method of empowerment that would allow them to free their communities form its desperation and despair and to effectively wage the fight against unfairness, inequality, and injustice.

Mayor Jackson provided the fundamental under-standing that is so desperately needed in our state, local, and national leadership. Urban America feels powerless to make law enforcement agencies more responsive to the needs of the community. They feel powerless to close down the crack houses and stop the selling of drugs at their schools and in their streets. They feel helpless in finding jobs or starting their own businesses. They feel powerless at changing the unfair insurance and bank red-lining that continues to add to the pain of their struggle. The pain, frustration, and feelings of helplessness can only be overcome by empowering the consciousness of urban America. This requires that our political, civic, business, and educational leaders go to urban America to work hands on with the people. They must help them to develop the strategies and solutions to the problems of their communities and, empower them to effect change.

We must build community teams, facilitated by elected officials and/or those on their staffs who know how the government works and how to get things done. There are those who would argue that community-based programs have not been any more effective than other programs and that there has never been much success at getting the people who live in urban America to work together. However, further analysis of these failed efforts reveals that we don't spend enough time and energy on the foundation building. Earlier, when I examined the failure of trickle-down economics, I stated that we cannot build a house from the top down. The same holds true in the development of task forces and community coalitions in urban America.

In communities where the young don't respect the old, where neighbors don't speak to each other, where store owners don't respect their customers, and where law enforcement has a history of brutality against the community, we must first develop the foundation of mutual respect, understanding, and communication. Leadership and sensitivity training must precede coalition development. Workshops and forums must be presented where people are allowed to articulate their anger and frustration. People must have the opportunity to share their pain. Only after helping people reach the level where they can communicate their feelings in a positive and non-threatening way can we begin to help them see their neighbors as real people with real problems. Then we can begin to train them in the group dynamics of working together.

We must teach people how to listen to the problems, concerns, and needs of each other. Major corporations know that despite employing some of the most educated and experienced people with the best and brightest minds, project teams and task forces are often ineffective until employees are trained in group dynamics and how to work together. Public education which has historically encouraged and celebrated individual achievement has not prepared people to work together. Thus, companies are retraining their employees. Teaching them how to work together and how to encourage input from their coworkers, in effect, how to build a team. Employees are being taught how to create an atmosphere where everyone is encouraged to discuss the problems that are important to them individually and to develop solutions that attempt to satisfy everyone's needs.

Programs in the past have failed because we have simply thrown a bunch of people together without preparing them to work together. We have not empowered them to bring any real and lasting change. And we have not given them someone in business or government who will effectively lobby on their behalf.

We have offered them no preparation, no solutions, no plans, no programs, and no way out.

Chapter 9

The special implications for black America

Black America felt a pain twisting at its insides with each not guilty verdict reached in the Rodney King case. Those within our community not given to violence cried. Each tear carried fading hopes for a judicial system which would treat us fairly and justly. Many in our community said enough is enough. The rage and frustration had become overwhelming. They remembered the words of Malcolm X, "by any means necessary." There was so much anger in black America that the church-goers, the elite, the middle class, the lost, the forgotten, and the hopelessly abandoned suddenly found themselves inextricably tied together in their feelings of frustration and rage.

Although we didn't all agree with the violence, although we didn't all agree on directing their anger at the Koreans, white pedestrians and business owners, most of us understood the rage that drove them to do it.

Not since Dr. Martin Luther King, Jr. led the march on Washington has a single event caused so many within our community to talk about working together. The gangs are talking about putting their differences behind them and gathering their collective strength. They're talking about redirecting their energy from terrorizing our communities to rebuilding it. Businessmen are talking about investing in our communities. They're talking about providing jobs and encouraging entrepreneurship. Blacks in corporate America who have developed the management and marketing skills needed to build viable and successful businesses are talking about working together to start businesses and provide pride and opportunity for young blacks previously abandoned in our inner cities. Corporate executives, entertainers, and athletes are talking about redirecting their collective, enormous wealth into black businesses and into buying back the property within the black community. Our churches and community organizations are talking about harnessing our voting power to demand governmental support in building programs that address the needs of our inner cities, programs that help to break the endless cycle of hopelessness and despair.

Yes, this event has us talking.

But we have talked about what we were going to do before. We have talked about registering to vote. We have talked about working together. We have talked about supporting each other. We have talked about taking ownership of, and responsibility for, our communities. Yet the trend continues in our communities where those of us who are capable leave, and those who stay do so because they are stuck there.

We are angry at the Koreans and other non-black-owned businesses because of their high prices, inferior products, and their openly blatant mistreatment of black customers. We are angry at the liquor and tobacco industry targeting our community for their legalized drugs. We are angry at the athletic shoe companies who target our young men in advertising their ridiculously overpriced sneakers. Too many in our community have been brainwashed into believing that a drink or a smoke will remove their pain. Too many of our young men are willing to kill for sneakers that they can't afford because of advertising that has brainwashed them into believing that only by wearing certain shoes will their young lives have real value. Our children are being taught that the American dream only awaits those black and minority children who can run fast, jump high, throw a football, or dunk a basketball.

Noticeably missing from the advertising of those who target our community are the positive images of black doctors, lawyers, accountants, business people, educators, engineers, and scientists. The images before our children teach them that the only successful blacks who eat Wheaties, drink Coca Cola, and drive automobiles are athletes and entertainers. The subliminal message that our children receive is that the only blacks who have value in this society are athletes and entertainers.

Yet, we allow others to profit from and to perpetuate the pain of urban America in general and the black community in particular. We fail to effectively and systematically organize our enormous purchasing power. We continue to allow the media and advertisers to define who we are. No one forces us to patronize businesses that disrespect us. No one forces us to patronize businesses that won't hire our young people. We have talked about consciously supporting our own businesses or at least those responding to the needs of our community, but we have failed to make that talk a part of our collective consciousness.

Few within our community can proudly claim their needs are being serviced by a black accountant, lawyer, dentist, and doctor. Few within our community can claim services at black-owned cleaners, pharmacies, grocery stores, and gas stations. We occasionally venture into a soul food restaurant, black-owned McDonald's, or night club. But we won't tip black waiters, waitresses, and bartenders to the same extent as we do others. Too often when our people serve us, in our minds they can't do anything right, whereas we overlook the poor service we receive from others. One bad experience with a black accountant, attorney, or black-owned business is enough for many of us to never do business with other blacks again.

Our students at the historically black colleges are not being prepared for, or encouraged to pursue entrepreneurship, reinvestment, or the ownership of businesses in black communities. Without developing programs and support mechanisms that teach these, the best and brightest minds in our community, how to develop the businesses, products, and resources to rebuild our community, another generation of frustration awaits us. With our community spending billions of dollars annually, with only a fraction of that enormous wealth being spent with black-owned businesses, we must prepare our children to recognize and take advantage of this extraordinary opportunity. We must teach them how to channel their extraordinary energy into economic and community empowerment.

We must rethink the rationale of sending our sons and daughters to college, particularly majority universities, spending anywhere from $20,000 to $100,000 for an education that prepares them to get a $30,000 per year job that keeps them too busy to get involved in the issues that are threatening to destroy their communities! And, should they lose their corporate job, where they continue to be the last hired and the first fired, they are ill-prepared to do anything else. The unemployment offices are full of college graduates standing alongside high school dropouts.

Our churches must more openly encourage, support, and provide the mechanisms for their congregations to support each other and to invest in themselves and their own communities. They must more effectively build the bridge between the varying social, economic, and educational levels of those within their congregations and within the communities surrounding their churches. Historically the African-American church has been the focal point of the efforts for social change and civil rights within the black community. The church must realize its role in bridging the gap and bringing together our community to provide mentors, networking, and a sharing of the resources and information needed to achieve community empowerment. The church represents the one place where black educators, business people, political leaders, welfare recipients, white and blue collar, young and old gather together. It is historically the one place in our community where spiritual empowerment bridges the gap between people of differing social, educational, and economic levels. It is the place where single mothers can connect with retired educators who can lobby in our public schools on behalf of our children. The place where those who understand the political process can mobilize community leaders to action. The place where our children, who are being drawn into gangs, drugs, violence, and teenage pregnancies, can connect with experienced and successful blacks who can become their mentors providing them with desperately needed advice and counseling.

Our professional organizations, fraternities, and sororities must develop the collective consciousness and employ effective strategies in using their enormous purchasing and voting power to lobby corporate America and our elected officials to support community empowerment.

They who are the intellectually and financially elite of our community must not allow themselves individually, and their organizations collectively, to become disconnected from our community. Each year black professional organizations spend billions or dollars in support of their national, regional, and local meetings. They must increase their awareness and raise the consciousness of their respective organizations to question who owns the hotel or meeting place. Do they advertise in black publications? Do they support historically black colleges? Do they contribute to scholarship programs for our young people? What are their relations with black employees, or do they even employ blacks? Too many of the hotels and convention centers hire blacks to clean the rooms and the tables but do not employ them in the decision making and hiring positions or in the roles of waitresses and bartenders who profit from the thousands of dollars we indiscriminately leave in tips. Their relationship with our community is one way. They take the millions of dollars that we spend with them and they run away!

Conference planners frequently organize tours and shopping sprees, few of which provide their attendees with the opportunity to do business with black-owned businesses. Exhibit planners frequently treat minority vendors with disregard and disrespect. They treat them as unwanted peddlers who they charge exorbitant exhibit fees while relegating them to rooms that are too small and locations so far removed from their meeting rooms that conference attendees must journey upstairs or downstairs, around the corner, or in the basement to find them. Not only do they fail to encourage their attendees to support their own businesses, their conference agenda schedules meetings so close together that attendees have little time to patronize those businesses who are part of the life-blood of our community. It is not uncommon to go into an exhibit area and find our educational and professional elite bickering with a black vendor over a few dollars while never questioning the white-owned hotel over the exorbitant price of the rooms, room service, and liquor. As conference planners walk through the exhibit area and see black vendors making money for themselves, their families, and their communities, they think, "if they (the vendors) are making so much money off of our attendees we should charge them more next year." Yet they fail to apply the same reasoning to Nike, Ford, General Motors, Budweiser, Michelob, Coca Cola, Hyatt, Marriott, and Sheraton who profit far more from our community than the few dollars made by these small black vendors. We cannot continue to break the backs of our own businesses and demand little from those businesses that are making billions of dollars off of our community.

As we journey to our conferences and conventions we fail to raise the question of whether the travel agencies and hotel transportation services are black-owned. Do the airlines or hotels contribute any of the millions of dollars that we spend to scholarship programs for our children? Do they contribute in any way to the uplifting of our communities?

In the major airports that I have travelled into, I have never been aware of a black-owned van or airport transportation service. Many, however, do have black-owned/operated taxis. The van services are a few dollars cheaper. Yet it is the black taxis drivers, together with their families, who are struggling to survive in a racist and oppressive society. But with whom do we spend our money?

Many of our elite boast of their Hispanic housekeepers and Asian gardeners, because they do a better job than blacks? Doesn't that remind you of how we used to say that the white man's ice was colder than the black man's ice?

Many of our entertainers and athletes don't have black agents, attorneys, investment bankers, or real estate brokers. They don't deposit money in black-owned banks. They don't shop with black-owned clothing stores. They don't use black-owned caterers for their many parties and social gatherings. They don't use black-owned printers or party planners. As a matter of fact, the more money they make the fewer blacks that are a part of their world. Some would say it's simply a matter of choice. I say it's a matter of conscience or, more accurately, consciousness.

In workshops that I present on community empowerment, I raise the question, "How much did you spend for everything that you are wearing today (e.g., shirt, pants, shoes, jewelry, perfume, etc.)? Now add to that what you paid for your car, your house, furniture, etc." The total for most people is staggering. But even more staggering is their answer to the next question. "How much of that was spent with black-owned businesses? Was your home brought or sold through a black real estate broker? Was your mortgage financed through a black bank? Was your automobile purchased through a black salesperson or from a black-owned dealership? Was your auto, home, and life insurance purchased from black agents?"

Few of our professional elite maintain their lavish offices in black-owned buildings. They don't use black-owned printers, graphic artists, illustrators, or couriers. They don't mentor young blacks by providing jobs and training opportunities. Like white America, they are looking for "the best qualified for the job." A song that's been sung to us by others is now being sung to us by our own community.

Television, of which we watch a lot of, has preciously few blacks on screen or behind the scenes. We see few blacks being paid to model in the print ads and in commercials promoting the many products that we purchase. The exceptions of course are those companies who spend millions of dollars targeting us for their advertisements for liquor, cigarettes, and sneakers.

We continue to spend much and demand little from those profiting from our community and the many more who profit from our pain.

More and more of us have turned away from the black church. We complain about how our churches no longer address the needs of the community. We complain of how we are no longer in need of preaching but are in need of teaching. We cannot, however, avoid the reality that if our churches are failing our community, it is because we are failing to make them work. We must stop blaming others for what they are not doing and ask ourselves what we have done. If all of black America tithed 10 percent of its income to our churches, gave regularly to our colleges and community organizations, and contributed its time, talents, and resources to the empowerment and uplifting of our community, we would resolve many of the problems that threaten to destroy our community.

The issue is not whether America has abandoned us but whether we have abandoned ourselves.

Enough is enough.

Chapter 10

What we must do

We must elect leaders who, together with their staffs, will work to develop a better understanding of the problems and cultural diversities of urban America. We must recognize those people who would prey on our fears and prejudices as they try to convince us that the solutions to America's urban problems are simply building more jails, locking up more people, and filling our streets with more insensitive policemen. Selecting the proper leadership is the necessary first step in setting the tone in state, local, and federal government that the problems of our inner cities are real American problems which affect all of the American people. Regardless of whether those who live in urban America are black, white, Latino, Asian, or other minorities we must all share in the commitment to ease their pain and have the will to help resolve their problems.

Personal and Community Empowerment

Programs and solutions must be directed toward achieving the long-term goals of personal and community empowerment. Much is said about the urban poor moving themselves off of welfare, finding jobs, starting businesses, and developing stronger families. We demand that they more effectively build character and teach morality to their children. However, a welfare consciousness does not become a self-help and wealth consciousness without education. Bad parents don't become good parents without training. Dysfunctional families don't become strong fully functional families without people, programs, and the community working to pull the family together. Helpless people don't become empowered people without a spiritual and emotional uplifting.

Our approach must be holistically directed at building the people and communities from the inside out. We must strengthen the foundation by building the spirit, character, and consciousness.

Conflict resolution and stress management have found their way into the work place as companies have witnessed chronically depressed emotionally enraged white and blue collar workers kill fellow employees, their families, and themselves. The urban poor, and those resigned to welfare who have never held jobs, are also in desperate need of being taught how to cope. For years urban America's black on black crime has taken the lives of our mothers and fathers, sons and daughters, friends and relatives. The hundreds of daily poor and minority victims of the rage in urban America are seen as merely statistics on our nightly newscasts. Left to themselves to cope with their own problems, resolved their own conflicts, and find a release from their stress.

We must strengthen the urban family to cope with their stress, anger, and frustration. We must take a more aggressive and proactive stance against child and spouse abuse. Battered women and abused children must have more options than simply filing criminal complaints. We shake our heads and pity battered wives. We vigorously pursue removing children from abusive households to place them into an already over-burdened Foster Care system. Think America! We must stop simply applying band-aids to urban America's mental health problems and throwing those who can't cope in jail. We must become proactive in helping to develop the mental health and emotional stability of families before they explode.

We must infuse conflict resolution and stress management training into our classrooms. Our children are in need of developing effective interpersonal and communication skills. We cannot continue to expel young black and Latino boys from our classrooms, relegating them to behavioral disorder and special education classes. Instead of helping them to resolve their problems and to understand their anger we are placing them on track to become the next generation of high school dropouts and urban terrorists. We cannot avoid the reality that our children are angry and are in need of discussing their feelings and must be taught how to cope with the many conflicts that they encounter daily. Teachers must be taught how to recognize the danger signals and how to respond to the anger and frustration of urban children.

Conflict resolution classes must become an integral part of the public school curriculum and mandated in our juvenile delinquency programs. They, together with stress training should also be made mandatory for those collecting welfare.

Before heads of households can be moved from welfare into the work force, accessibility to Head Start and affordability of health care must be made available. The physical, emotional, and mental health of families must be developed. A healthier generation of children will be born to mothers who have easier access to, and mandatory participation in, prenatal clinical care.

Welfare and unemployment benefits should be designed to sustain families while they move from unemployment into the work force or into entrepreneurship. Qualification for benefits should be based on whole-family needs and not encourage the break-up of the nuclear family by being restricted to single-parent households.

Job training programs must be mandated through both welfare and social service programs and designed to move people off of welfare into jobs. Parent training must be mandated to help parents develop effective parenting skills, to better help their children cope with the added stress of growing up in urban America, to teach morality and to build the character that will help them to become valuable and contributing members of this society.

Workshop and training program attendance, together with available job acceptance, must become mandatory for continued welfare benefits.

Head Start programs for preschoolers and after school programs for school-age children must be made available to all families so that in two parent homes, both parents will be available for education and retraining for work and careers that will lead to economic empowerment.

Motivational and inspirational programs must be offered to empower the consciousness of those who feel themselves hopelessness trapped. Many have lost the spirit and the will to succeed. They are in need of spiritual empowerment and inspirational enlightenment. They must have a vision before they can develop a plan. Like many in America, they are in need of a spiritual renewal.

The mentality of people on welfare is not all that different from people who have jobs. By that I mean that the average employee doesn't go to work every day looking for new and better ways to do his or her job. He or she doesn't wake up each morning with the insatiable desire to learn new skills. The average employee doesn't have the consciousness to go to the bookstore or to the library to read books on how to become a better writer, speaker, thinker, planner, strategist, etc. If he or she is having problems with their marriage, raising their children, communicating with their management, or managing their credit, they aren't running down to the local bookstore or registering for courses at the local community college to acquire the knowledge to overcome their problem areas. In fact, if companies told their employees that they could stay home and still get paid most people wouldn't go to work. And those who did would eventually become resentful of those who didn't and would ultimately stay home as well.

Thus, under our current system of welfare we are in effect telling people that they can stay at home and still get paid. And instead of systematically helping them to develop the consciousness to do better for themselves we give them just enough to survive on while making their lives miserable, trapping them and their children in poverty. The misery and poverty of urban America has trapped families for generations.

We must understand and accept the reality that many of those on welfare want a better life for themselves and their families. Their problem is that they don't know what to do. People who have never owned a business don't know how to start a business. People who have never gone to a job interview don't know how to dress, speak, and prepare to present themselves. People who lack self-esteem and self-confidence, who have experienced little success in their lives don't know how to define their goals and develop action plans. These people are in need of consciousness raising and personal development. Much of their world is comprised of people who, like themselves, have broken spirits and crushed dreams. We must help them develop their spirits and their self-confidence through workshops and seminars presented by people who have climbed up from where they are. It's these personal testimonies and real life stories that help people to see a light at the end of the tunnel and to develop action plans that they feel capable of implementing.

Community empowerment is interwoven within the educational and economic empowerment of communities. Communities should be trained in developing community-based credit unions to provide for the banking and credit needs of community residents. These credit unions would be owned and operated by community residents. They would be responsible for providing workshops and seminars pertinent to community needs such as how to apply for personal and business loans or how to open savings and checking accounts.

Low priced homes, low interest loans, and other incentives should be used to encourage home ownership. Training programs should help people develop the skills to work on the construction team to assist in building their own home or to renovate the run down buildings in their communities giving them practical skills and self-pride. The laws should be strengthened making it more difficult for scam artists and fraudulent mortgage brokers to prey on uneducated and uninformed people. Before contracts can be held binding and homes foreclosed, the burden of proof must shift to the scam artists and their obscure contracts making it more difficult for them to con people out of their homes.

A Mandate for the Rights of American Citizens

The President must mandate that the federal government vigorously pursue civil rights violations. America must become intolerant of housing and job discrimination and sexual bias and harassment. Too many in urban America painfully struggle to uplift themselves only to find themselves sexually harassed or discriminated against in jobs and housing. They survive the gangs and violence of urban America only to become the victims of hate crimes in suburban America.

The accountability of civil rights violations by law enforcement agencies must be expanded to not only hold responsible those directly involved but those in leadership who perpetuate an environment which condones racism, sexism, and prejudice.

A Mandate for Public Education

The American public education system must develop a curriculum which focuses on whole-child development. The curriculum must be expanded to teach cultural diversity, character, morality, tolerance and understanding of the different ethnicities which make up America. Each classroom in each school must become a field of dreams. The first day of school each student must be encouraged to develop a dream. The school environment, classroom organization and teacher and staff attitudes must be developed to support and encourage achievement of those dreams.

The teaching methodologies and core curriculum must be made relevant to the lives of the children in the school. The curriculum of urban children requires a special focus on the problems of urban America. Urban children must become empowered with an understanding of, and insight into, the issues, politics, and history of urban ghettos in America. They must be taught the critical thinking skills needed to effectively identify and debate the problems confronting their communities and to the solutions needed to rebuild and uplift their communities.

In urban communities particularly, discussions of character, morality, and discipline must be made first in the cultural context of the students and secondly in the context of achieving their dreams and empowering their communities. Dreaming brings about vision, which brings about direction, which determines actions.

We cannot deny the fact that public schools provide the first model of what our children can expect from America. If their schools are allowed to decay, their hallways to become dirty, their paint to become dull, their books and materials to become dilapidated, then our children will come to believe that this is all that America will offer them. Not opportunity but abandonment. Not preparing them to compete in a highly competitive world but to become helplessly and hopelessly trapped in urban America. To understand how parents and students feel about their schools and those teaching them we should perform an annual survey. This is a necessary first step in the direction of holding public education responsible to the public.

Federal, state, and local elected officials should sponsor community town hall meetings. These would provide opportunities for community residents to meet face to face in a forum to voice their concerns with those elected to serve them.

The Public Education - Business Partnership

The business community, particularly those who have succeeded against the odds with their roots in urban America, must direct more money into scholarships and school support programs. Schools should be taught how to solicit support and sponsorship from the business community for their uniforms, equipment, supplies and materials. Communities should be taught how to more effectively encourage business involvement in their schools. Urban parents and children have enormous purchasing power which is targeted by the billions of dollars in advertising directed at them. Parents and students must be taught how to redirect their attention and focus their support toward those companies who are supporting their schools.

More people from the private sector must be encouraged to spend quality time with students in schools and in classrooms where they can share with them the invaluable strategies and skills that are needed to succeed. Providing students with a holistic look at their careers, their lives, and their experiences. People from industry, who have hands on experience at building businesses, recruiting teams, developing business plans, and achieving business goals are the best qualified to teach these concepts to students.

Corporate America should develop payroll deduction plans that encourages and simplifies the way for employees to make regular contributions to their primary and secondary schools. Departments within the company should be encouraged to participate in adopt-a-school programs. This is the type of corporate leadership needed move education to the forefront of the American corporate agenda.

Develop Community Partnerships

We must teach communities how to develop a partnership between urban schools, law enforcement agencies, local government, community businesses, and community churches. It is this partnership of working together that rekindles the spirit of urban America and provides hope for developing solutions to the multitude of problems facing its people.

Many of the people who live in urban America have the desire and the work ethic to become good employees and successful entrepreneurs. They are lacking job skills in many of the emerging industries and technologies. They also lack accessibility to training in the areas of their natural abilities. Many have the physical skills for labor intensive work such as street repair and construction. Others have the creative skills for such work as illustrators, graphic artists, and architects. And still others have and the patience and compassion for teaching, social work, Head Start, and work with juveniles. Business plans and mentors should be provided to those who have the desire and are willing to make the commitment to build a successful business. We must educate people and provide the appropriate training and support to move them from welfare and dead end jobs into businesses and careers that are consistent with their natural abilities and intrinsic desires.

A broad reaching and effective plan of investment incentives must be developed to encourage investment in our inner cities. Programs must provide incentives for companies to open stores, manufacturing facilities, and offices in urban communities. Essential to such programs would be the requirement that companies give preferential treatment in hiring and training people from within the community. Welfare and social service training programs should be directed at those skill areas needed by local employers.

Companies must be given incentives to become mentors and sponsor programs to assist community residents in developing community-based businesses. Companies should have a long-term employee development plan designed to move community residents through entry level employment into management training programs. From those management positions they should be trained and encouraged to pursue store ownership. Financial assistance and start-up capital should be set aside within the organization to support community-based business ownership. Repayment of such start-up capital could be taken from future store revenues. Many of urban America's most successful franchise operators have been groomed through programs like these.

Businesses should have incentives to purchase raw materials, supplies, support, and professional services from within the community. When support services and materials are not available locally, a joint partnership between business and government should provide the training, business planning, and start-up capital for community residents to pursue those businesses.

More skill training programs must be designed to

encourage entrepreneurship in the full spectrum of businesses that are viable to the community. Community residents should be trained to develop such businesses as grocery stores, clothing stores, dry cleaners, and other services supported by community residents. New government and industry related jobs that are performed in the community should be made available to residents of the community. A jobs data bank of community residents should be developed and drawn from. Community residents should be trained in job skill areas that will be needed in the community in the future. Community residents should be put to work building their own houses, cleaning their own streets, policing their own communities, and putting out fires in their own communities.

Financial aid programs should be cosponsored between business and government for students who will commit to returning to their communities for community work or teaching for a specified period of time following college graduation.

Political Empowerment

A handbook of political office holders, their phone numbers, and office locations together with their respective areas of responsibility should be given to all community households following all major elections. Included in the handbook should be key numbers to law enforcement agencies to report drugs, gangs, and any criminal activity occurring in the community. Workshops on how to make government work for the community should be provided to community residents. Community teams should be established to voice and to address community concerns. Teams should be made up of the staff persons of local political leaders together with a cross-section of community residents and law enforcement representatives.

Mock public forums on issues and legislative proposals should be held in public schools prior to public debate to stimulate awareness within the community. The magnitude of illiteracy in America requires that all legislative proposals, ballot initiatives, rezoning, and other important issues relating to communities be debated in town hall style meetings. Such meetings should be held at public school sites. This would provide parents, community leaders, business people, and elected officials with a hands on look at the buildings and communities where we are educating our children.

All elected officials should be required by law to hold these meetings on a regular basis in the communities from which they have been elected to serve. This will provide a forum for community residents to come face to face with all of their elected officials as well as those who have differing opinions who may be seeking elected office.

Community Policing

Community policing must be mandated in the most crime-ridden urban areas. Police and sheriff department substations should be located in the areas of the highest crime rates as opposed to the areas that have the most powerful lobbyists. Establish community crime watch coalitions and community patrols giving people a vested interest and active role in reclaiming their communities. Better publicize the reward and incentive programs available for those providing information and evidence leading to the conviction of those committing drug dealing and other violent crimes as well as those committing welfare, insurance, and tax fraud.

The federal forfeiture law allowing law enforcement agencies to take the property of people suspected of crimes should be repelled. This law has been abused by law enforcement agencies particularly in urban America and has amounted to nothing more than legalized extortion by the federal, state, and local government. Ironically, Washington, D.C. has become a tragic example of abuse of this statue. Police officers have used their power under this law to indiscriminately stop and search minorities legally confiscating (stealing) their money and property.

This law allows police to indiscriminately confiscate the money and property of people who they simply suspected of criminal activity. After the property has been confiscated, those suspected must hire an attorney and go through the complicated and expensive legal process to have their case heard so that they can prove that they had legally purchased the property or legally earned the money that was taken from them. Not only must they be financially and intellectually prepared to fight the government for the return of their property but even the most affluent can wind up financially ruined after attorney's fees and court costs.

Those from urban America who lack the education and financial resources to fight for the return of their property are simply left frustrated, angry, helpless and alone. Powerless to defend themselves they have become helpless victims in the hands of racist, dishonest, and abusive law enforcement and government officials. This ridiculous law has placed America at risk and urban America in even greater danger!

To help local law enforcement employees better understand, and to become better connected with, the communities that they serve they should be given incentives to live in those communities. Home ownership assistance, promotion and pay incentives should encourage police to live in the communities that they patrol. This is a significant step in helping those in law enforcement to understand the culture, problems, and pain of the communities which they serve.

Structural Rebuilding

Put community residents to work rebuilding their communities. Move those from welfare, county jails, and juvenile authorities into work programs to repaint defaced buildings, demolish condemned buildings, clean-up city streets and vacant lots, and renovate the structurally sound but decaying buildings. Focus ongoing attention to such aesthetic and safety areas as street repaving, pest and trash control, street light and sidewalk repair, and landscaping.

Program Implementation Mandates

The legislative process of implementing community programs must be limited to a specifically defined time frame. A budget should be established and published. As mentioned before, each community must have a community team derived from the community partnership. The community team should work to develop a community plan that would be presented to the appropriate elected official. If the legislative process fails to develop a by-partisan plan by the legislative deadline, the community plan must be implemented for the next fiscal year.

We must stop blaming those who are trapped in desperate and hopeless situations as being solely responsible for their dilemma. Urban America must be given an opportunity to define its own destiny and not be held hostage by politicians who continue their endless discussions and debates about what to do. While we work to apply more critical thinking and moral conscience in debating the problems and developing the solutions to their problems we must empower them to work toward developing their own solutions. It does not make good sense, nor is it in good conscience, to deprive our schools of the resources to properly educate American children when we have the evidence of the cost of crime and prisons to the American people. It makes no business sense for corporate America to lend a deaf ear to the problems of urban America when so much of their revenue is derived from urban communities and those who have ties to urban communities.

We cannot fail to commit the resources to empowering urban America no more than we can avoid the responsibility of shaping the character and morality of our children. If we do not provide dreams and vision to those who are feeling lost and forgotten, we are playing Russian roulette with our society. Bullets have no names and we are all at risk of being caught in the next explosion.

Urban America has issued America a painful wake-up call. Is America listening?